Marmion

Marmion

A Tale of Flodden Field

Sir Walter Scott

MINT EDITIONS

Marmion: A Tale of Flodden Field was first published in 1817.

This edition published by Mint Editions 2021.

ISBN 9781513280332 | E-ISBN 9781513285351

Published by Mint Editions®

MINT
EDITIONS

minteditionbooks.com

Publishing Director: Jennifer Newens
Design & Production: Rachel Lopez Metzger
Project Manager: Micaela Clark
Typesetting: Westchester Publishing Services

November's sky is chill and drear,
November's leaf is red and sear:
Late, gazing down the steepy linn
That hems our little garden in,
Low in its dark and narrow glen
You scarce the rivulet might ken,
So thick the tangled greenwood grew,
So feeble thrilled the streamlet through:
Now, murmuring hoarse, and frequent seen
Through bush and briar, no longer green,
An angry brook, it sweeps the glade,
Brawls over rock and wild cascade,
And foaming brown, with doubled speed,
Hurries its waters to the Tweed.

    No longer Autumn's glowing red
Upon our forest hills is shed;
No more, beneath the evening beam,
Fair Tweed reflects their purple gleam:
Away hath passed the heather-bell
That bloomed so rich on Needpath Fell;
Sallow his brow, and russet bare
Are now the sister-heights of Yair.
The sheep, before the pinching heaven,
To sheltered dale and down are driven,
Where yet some faded herbage pines,
And yet a watery sunbeam shines:
In meek despondency they eye
The withered sward and wintry sky,
And far beneath their summer hill,
Stray sadly by Glenkinnon's rill:
The shepherd shifts his mantle's fold,
And wraps him closer from the cold;
His dogs no merry circles wheel,
But, shivering, follow at his heel;
A cowering glance they often cast,
As deeper moans the gathering blast.

My imps, though hardy, bold, and wild,
As best befits the mountain child,
Feel the sad influence of the hour,
And wail the daisy's vanished flower;
Their summer gambols tell, and mourn,
And anxious ask: "Will spring return,
And birds and lambs again be gay,
And blossoms clothe the hawthorn spray?"

Yes, prattlers, yes. The daisy's flower
Again shall paint your summer bower;
Again the hawthorn shall supply
The garlands you delight to tie;
The lambs upon the lea shall bound,
The wild birds carol to the round,
And while you frolic light as they,
Too short shall seem the summer day.

To mute and to material things
New life revolving summer brings;
The genial call dead Nature hears,
And in her glory reappears.
But oh! my country's wintry state
What second spring shall renovate?
What powerful call shall bid arise
The buried warlike and the wise;
The mind that thought for Britain's weal,
The hand that grasped the victor steel?
The vernal sun new life bestows
Even on the meanest flower that blows;
But vainly, vainly may he shine,
Where glory weeps o'er Nelson's shrine;
And vainly pierce the solemn gloom,
That shrouds, O Pitt, thy hallowed tomb!

Deep graved in every British heart,
Oh never let those names depart!
Say to your sons—Lo, here his grave,
Who victor died on Gadite wave;

To him, as to the burning levin,
Short, bright, resistless course was given.
Where'er his country's foes were found,
Was heard the fated thunder's sound,
Till burst the bolt on yonder shore,
Rolled, blazed, destroyed—and was no more.

Nor mourn ye less his perished worth,
Who bade the conqueror go forth,
And launched that thunderbolt of war
On Egypt, Hafnia, Trafalgar;
Who, born to guide such high emprize,
For Britain's weal was early wise;
Alas! to whom the Almighty gave,
For Britain's sins, an early grave!
His worth, who, in his mightiest hour,
A bauble held the pride of power,
Spurned at the sordid lust of pelf,
And served his Albion for herself;
Who, when the frantic crowd amain
Strained at subjection's bursting rein,
O'er their wild mood full conquest gained,
The pride he would not crush restrained,
Showed their fierce zeal a worthier cause,
And brought the freeman's arm to aid the freeman's laws.

Hadst thou but lived, though stripped of power,
A watchman on the lonely tower,
Thy thrilling trump had roused the land,
When fraud or danger were at hand;
By thee, as by the beacon-light,
Our pilots had kept course aright;
As some proud column, though alone,
Thy strength had propped the tottering throne:
Now is the stately column broke,
The beacon-light is quenched in smoke,
The trumpet's silver sound is still,
The warder silent on the hill!

Oh think, how to his latest day,
When Death, just hovering, claimed his prey,
With Palinure's unaltered mood,
Firm at his dangerous post he stood;
Each call for needful rest repelled,
With dying hand the rudder held,
Till in his fall, with fateful sway,
The steerage of the realm gave way!
Then, while on Britain's thousand plains
One unpolluted church remains,
Whose peaceful bells ne'er sent around
The bloody tocsin's maddening sound,
But still, upon the hallowed day,
Convoke the swains to praise and pray;
While faith and civil peace are dear,
Grace this cold marble with a tear—
He who preserved them, Pitt, lies here!

Nor yet suppress the generous sigh,
Because his rival slumbers nigh;
Nor be thy *requiescat* dumb,
Lest it be said o'er Fox's tomb.
For talents mourn, untimely lost
When best employed, and wanted most;
Mourn genius high, and lore profound,
And wit that loved to play, not wound;
And all the reasoning powers divine,
To penetrate, resolve, combine;
And feelings keen, and fancy's glow—
They sleep with him who sleeps below:
And if thou mourn'st they could not save
From error him who owns this grave,
Be every harsher thought suppressed,
And sacred be the last long rest.
Here, where the end of earthly things
Lays heroes, patriots, bards, and kings;
Where stiff the hand, and still the tongue,
Of those who fought, and spoke, and sung;
Here, where the fretted aisles prolong

The distant notes of holy song,
As if some angel spoke again,
"All peace on earth, goodwill to men;"
If ever from an English heart,
Oh, *here* let prejudice depart,
And, partial feeling cast aside,
Record that Fox a Briton died!
When Europe crouched to France's yoke,
And Austria bent, and Prussia broke,
And the firm Russian's purpose brave
Was bartered by a timorous slave,
Even then dishonour's peace he spurned,
The sullied olive-branch returned,
Stood for his country's glory fast,
And nailed her colours to the mast!
Heaven, to reward his firmness, gave
A portion in this honoured grave,
And ne'er held marble in its trust
Of two such wondrous men the dust.

With more than mortal powers endowed,
How high they soared above the crowd!
Theirs was no common party race,
Jostling by dark intrigue for place;
Like fabled gods, their mighty war
Shook realms and nations in its jar;
Beneath each banner proud to stand,
Looked up the noblest of the land,
Till through the British world were known
The names of Pitt and Fox alone.
Spells of such force no wizard grave
E'er framed in dark Thessalian cave,
Though his could drain the ocean dry,
And force the planets from the sky,
These spells are spent, and, spent with these,
The wine of life is on the lees.
Genius, and taste, and talent gone,
For ever tombed beneath the stone,
Where—taming thought to human pride!—

The mighty chiefs sleep side by side.
Drop upon Fox's grave the tear,
'Twill trickle to his rival's bier;
O'er Pitt's the mournful requiem sound,
And Fox's shall the notes rebound.
The solemn echo seems to cry—
"Here let their discord with them die.
Speak not for those a separate doom,
Whom Fate made brothers in the tomb;
But search the land of living men,
Where wilt thou find their like again?"

Rest, ardent spirits! till the cries
Of dying Nature bid you rise;
Not even your Britain's groans can pierce
The leaden silence of your hearse;
Then, oh, how impotent and vain
This grateful tributary strain!
Though not unmarked, from northern clime,
Ye heard the Border minstrel's rhyme
His Gothic harp has o'er you rung;
The bard you deigned to praise, your deathless names has sung.

Stay yet, illusion, stay a while,
My wildered fancy still beguile!
From this high theme how can I part,
Ere half unloaded is my heart!
For all the tears e'er sorrow drew,
And all the raptures fancy knew,
And all the keener rush of blood,
That throbs through bard in bardlike mood,
Were here a tribute mean and low,
Though all their mingled streams could flow—
Woe, wonder, and sensation high,
In one spring-tide of ecstasy!
It will not be—it may not last—
The vision of enchantment's past:
Like frostwork in the morning ray
The fancied fabric melts away;

Each Gothic arch, memorial-stone,
And long, dim, lofty aisle, are gone;
And lingering last, deception dear,
The choir's high sounds die on my ear.
Now slow return the lonely down,
The silent pastures bleak and brown,
The farm begirt with copsewood wild,
The gambols of each frolic child,
Mixing their shrill cries with the tone
Of Tweed's dark waters rushing on.

Prompt on unequal tasks to run,
Thus Nature disciplines her son:
Meeter, she says, for me to stray,
And waste the solitary day,
In plucking from yon fen the reed,
And watch it floating down the Tweed;
Or idly list the shrilling lay
With which the milkmaid cheers her way,
Marking its cadence rise and fail,
As from the field, beneath her pail,
She trips it down the uneven dale:
Meeter for me, by yonder cairn,
The ancient shepherd's tale to learn;
Though oft he stop in rustic fear,
Lest his old legends tire the ear
Of one who, in his simple mind,
May boast of book-learned taste refined.

But thou, my friend, canst fitly tell,
(For few have read romance so well)
How still the legendary lay
O'er poet's bosom holds its sway;
How on the ancient minstrel strain
Time lays his palsied hand in vain;
And how our hearts at doughty deeds,
By warriors wrought in steely weeds,
Still throb for fear and pity's sake;
As when the Champion of the Lake

Enters Morgana's fated house,
Or in the Chapel Perilous,
Despising spells and demons' force,
Holds converse with the unburied corse;
Or when, Dame Ganore's grace to move,
(Alas, that lawless was their love!)
He sought proud Tarquin in his den,
And freed full sixty knights; or when,
A sinful man, and unconfessed,
He took the Sangreal's holy quest,
And, slumbering, saw the vision high,
He might not view with waking eye.

The mightiest chiefs of British song
Scorned not such legends to prolong:
They gleam through Spenser's elfin dream,
And mix in Milton's heavenly theme;
And Dryden, in immortal strain,
Had raised the Table Round again,
But that a ribald king and court
Bade him toil on, to make them sport;
Demanded for their niggard pay,
Fit for their souls, a looser lay,
Licentious satire, song, and play;
The world defrauded of the high design,
Profaned the God-given strength, and marred the lofty line.

Warmed by such names, well may we then,
Though dwindled sons of little men,
Essay to break a feeble lance
In the fair fields of old romance;
Or seek the moated castle's cell,
Where long through talisman and spell,
While tyrants ruled, and damsels wept,
Thy Genius, Chivalry, hath slept:
There sound the harpings of the North,
Till he awake and sally forth,
On venturous quest to prick again,
In all his arms, with all his train,

Shield, lance, and brand, and plume, and scarf,
Fay, giant, dragon, squire, and dwarf,
And wizard with his want of might,
And errant maid on palfrey white.
Around the Genius weave their spells,
Pure Love, who scarce his passion tells;
Mystery, half veiled and half revealed;
And Honour, with his spotless shield;
Attention, with fixed eye; and Fear,
That loves the tale she shrinks to hear;
And gentle Courtesy; and Faith,
Unchanged by sufferings, time, or death;
And Valour, lion-mettled lord,
Leaning upon his own good sword.

Well has thy fair achievement shown
A worthy meed may thus be won;
Ytene's oaks—beneath whose shade
Their theme the merry minstrels made,
Of Ascapart, and Bevis bold,
And that Red King, who, while of old,
Through Boldrewood the chase he led,
By his loved huntsman's arrow bled—
Ytene's oaks have heard again
Renewed such legendary strain;
For thou hast sung how he of Gaul,
That Amadis so famed in hall,
For Oriana foiled in fight
The necromancer's felon might;
And well in modern verse hast wove
Partenopex's mystic love:
Hear, then, attentive to my lay,
A knightly tale of Albion's elder day.

Canto First

THE CASTLE

I

Day set on Norham's castled steep,
And Tweed's fair river, broad and deep,
    And Cheviot's mountains lone;
The battled towers, the donjon keep,
The loophole grates where captives weep,
The flanking walls that round it sweep,
    In yellow lustre shone.
The warriors on the turrets high,
Moving athwart the evening sky,
    Seemed forms of giant height:
Their armour, as it caught the rays,
Flashed back again the western blaze,
    In lines of dazzling light.

II

Saint George's banner, broad and gay,
Now faded, as the fading ray
    Less bright, and less, was flung;
The evening gale had scarce the power
To wave it on the donjon tower,
    So heavily it hung.
The scouts had parted on their search,
    The castle gates were barred;
Above the gloomy portal arch,
Timing his footsteps to a march,
    The warder kept his guard;
Low humming, as he paced along,
Some ancient Border gathering song.

III

A distant trampling sound he hears;
He looks abroad, and soon appears
O'er Horncliff Hill a plump of spears,
    Beneath a pennon gay;
A horseman, darting from the crowd,
Like lightning from a summer cloud,
Spurs on his mettled courser proud,
    Before the dark array.
Beneath the sable palisade
That closed the castle barricade,
    His bugle-horn he blew;
The warder hasted from the wall,
And warned the captain in the hall,
    For well the blast he knew;
And joyfully that knight did call,
To sewer, squire, and seneschal.

IV

"Now broach ye a pipe of Malvoisie,
    Bring pasties of the doe,
And quickly make the entrance free,
And bid my heralds ready be,
And every minstrel sound his glee,
    And all our trumpets blow;
And, from the platform, spare ye not
To fire a noble salvo-shot:
    Lord Marmion waits below!"
Then to the castle's lower ward
    Sped forty yeomen tall,
The iron-studded gates unbarred,
Raised the portcullis' ponderous guard,
The lofty palisade unsparred,
    And let the drawbridge fall.

V

Along the bridge Lord Marmion rode,
Proudly his red-roan charger trode,
His helm hung at the saddlebow;
Well by his visage you might know
He was a stalwart knight, and keen,
And had in many a battle been;
The scar on his brown cheek revealed
A token true of Bosworth field;
His eyebrow dark, and eye of fire,
Showed spirit proud and prompt to ire;
Yet lines of thought upon his cheek
Did deep design and counsel speak.
His forehead, by his casque worn bare,
His thick moustache, and curly hair,
Coal-black, and grizzled here and there,
    But more through toil than age;
His square-turned joints, and strength of limb,
Showed him no carpet knight so trim,
But in close fight a champion grim,
    In camps a leader sage.

VI

Well was he armed from head to heel,
In mail and plate of Milan steel;
But his strong helm, of mighty cost,
Was all with burnished gold embossed;
Amid the plumage of the crest,
A falcon hovered on her nest,
With wings outspread, and forward breast:
E'en such a falcon, on his shield,
Soared sable in an azure field:
The golden legend bore aright,
"Who checks at me, to death is dight."
Blue was the charger's broidered rein;
Blue ribbons decked his arching mane;

The knightly housing's ample fold
Was velvet blue, and trapped with gold.

VII

Behind him rode two gallant squires,
Of noble name and knightly sires:
They burned the gilded spurs to claim;
For well could each a war-horse tame,
Could draw the bow, the sword could sway,
And lightly bear the ring away;
Nor less with courteous precepts stored,
Could dance in hall, and carve at board,
And frame love-ditties passing rare,
And sing them to a lady fair.

VIII

Four men-at-arms came at their backs,
With halbert, bill, and battle-axe:
They bore Lord Marmion's lance so strong,
And led his sumpter-mules along,
And ambling palfrey, when at need
Him listed ease his battle-steed.
The last and trustiest of the four,
On high his forky pennon bore;
Like swallow's tail, in shape and hue,
Fluttered the streamer glossy blue,
Where, blazoned sable, as before,
The towering falcon seemed to soar.
Last, twenty yeomen, two and two,
In hosen black, and jerkins blue,
With falcons broidered on each breast,
Attended on their lord's behest:
Each, chosen for an archer good,
Knew hunting-craft by lake or wood;
Each one a six-foot bow could bend,
And far a clothyard shaft could send;

Each held a boar-spear tough and strong,
And at their belts their quivers rung.
Their dusty palfreys, and array,
Showed they had marched a weary way.

IX

'Tis meet that I should tell you now,
How fairly armed, and ordered how,
    The soldiers of the guard,
With musket, pike, and morion,
To welcome noble Marmion,
    Stood in the castle-yard;
Minstrels and trumpeters were there,
The gunner held his linstock yare,
    For welcome-shot prepared:
Entered the train, and such a clang,
As then through all his turrets rang,
    Old Norham never heard.

X

The guards their morrice-pikes advanced,
    The trumpets flourished brave,
The cannon from the ramparts glanced,
    And thundering welcome gave.
A blithe salute, in martial sort,
    The minstrels well might sound,
For, as Lord Marmion crossed the court,
    He scattered angels round.
"Welcome to Norham, Marmion!
    Stout heart, and open hand!
Well dost thou brook thy gallant roan,
    Thou flower of English land!"

XI

Two pursuivants, whom tabarts deck,
With silver scutcheon round their neck,

Stood on the steps of stone,
By which you reach the donjon gate,
And there, with herald pomp and state,
    They hailed Lord Marmion:
They hailed him Lord of Fontenaye,
Of Lutterward, and Scrivelbaye,
    Of Tamworth tower and town;
And he, their courtesy to requite,
Gave them a chain of twelve marks' weight,
    All as he lighted down.
"Now, largesse, largesse, Lord Marmion,
    Knight of the crest of gold!
A blazoned shield, in battle won,
    Ne'er guarded heart so bold."

XII

They marshalled him to the castle-hall,
    Where the guests stood all aside,
And loudly flourished the trumpet-call,
    And the heralds loudly cried—
"Room, lordlings, room for Lord Marmion,
    With the crest and helm of gold!
Full well we know the trophies won
    In the lists at Cottiswold:
There, vainly Ralph de Wilton strove
    'Gainst Marmion's force to stand;
To him he lost his lady-love,
    And to the king his land.
Ourselves beheld the listed field,
    A sight both sad and fair;
We saw Lord Marmion pierce his shield,
    And saw his saddle bare;
We saw the victor win the crest
    He wears with worthy pride;
And on the gibbet-tree, reversed,
    His foeman's scutcheon tied.
Place, nobles, for the Falcon-Knight!
    Room, room, ye gentles gay,

For him who conquered in the right,
    Marmion of Fontenaye!"

XIII

Then stepped, to meet that noble lord,
    Sir Hugh the Heron bold,
Baron of Twisell and of Ford,
    And captain of the hold.
He led Lord Marmion to the dais,
    Raised o'er the pavement high,
And placed him in the upper place—
    They feasted full and high:
The whiles a Northern harper rude
Chanted a rhyme of deadly feud,
    "How the fierce Thirwalls, and Ridleys all,
        Stout Willimondswick,
        And Hardriding Dick,
    And Hughie of Hawdon, and Will o' the Wall,
    Have set on Sir Albany Featherstonhaugh,
    And taken his life at the Deadman's-shaw."
Scantly Lord Marmion's ear could brook
    The harper's barbarous lay;
Yet much he praised the pains he took,
    And well those pains did pay:
For lady's suit and minstrel's strain,
By knight should ne'er be heard in vain.

XIV

"Now, good Lord Marmion," Heron says,
    "Of your fair courtesy,
I pray you bide some little space
    In this poor tower with me.
Here may you keep your arms from rust,
    May breathe your war-horse well;
Seldom hath passed a week but just
    Or feat of arms befell:
The Scots can rein a mettled steed,

And love to couch a spear;
St. George! a stirring life they lead,
    That have such neighbours near.
Then stay with us a little space,
    Our Northern wars to learn;
I pray you for your lady's grace!"
    Lord Marmion's brow grew stern.

XV

The captain marked his altered look,
    And gave a squire the sign;
A mighty wassail-bowl he took,
    And crowned it high with wine.
"Now pledge me here, Lord Marmion:
    But first I pray thee fair,
Where hast thou left that page of thine,
That used to serve thy cup of wine,
    Whose beauty was so rare?
When last in Raby towers we met,
    The boy I closely eyed,
And often marked his cheeks were wet,
    With tears he fain would hide:
His was no rugged horse-boy's hand,
To burnish shield or sharpen brand,
    Or saddle battle-steed;
But meeter seemed for lady fair,
To fan her cheek or curl her hair,
Or through embroidery, rich and rare,
    The slender silk to lead:
His skin was fair, his ringlets gold,
    His bosom—when he sighed—
The russet doublet's rugged fold
    Could scarce repel its pride!
Say, hast thou given that lovely youth
    To serve in lady's bower?
Or was the gentle page, in sooth,
    A gentle paramour?"

XVI

Lord Marmion ill could brook such jest;
    He rolled his kindling eye,
With pain his rising wrath suppressed,
    Yet made a calm reply:
"That boy thou thought'st so goodly fair,
He might not brook the Northern air.
More of his fate if thou wouldst learn,
I left him sick in Lindisfarne:
Enough of him. But, Heron, say,
Why does thy lovely lady gay
Disdain to grace the hall to-day?
Or has that dame, so fair and sage,
Gone on some pious pilgrimage?"
He spoke in covert scorn, for fame
Whispered light tales of Heron's dame.

XVII

Unmarked, at least unrecked, the taunt,
    Careless the knight replied,
"No bird whose feathers gaily flaunt
    Delights in cage to bide;
Norham is grim and grated close,
Hemmed in by battlement and fosse,
    And many a darksome tower;
And better loves my lady bright
To sit in liberty and light,
    In fair Queen Margaret's bower.
We hold our greyhound in our hand,
    Our falcon on our glove;
But where shall we find leash or band
    For dame that loves to rove?
Let the wild falcon soar her swing,
She'll stoop when she has tired her wing."

XVIII

"Nay, if with royal James's bride
  The lovely Lady Heron bide,
  Behold me here a messenger,
  Your tender greetings prompt to bear;
  For to the Scottish court addressed,
  I journey at our King's behest,
  And pray you, of your grace, provide
  For me and mine, a trusty guide.
  I have not ridden in Scotland since
  James backed the cause of that mock-prince,
  Warbeck, that Flemish counterfeit,
  Who on the gibbet paid the cheat.
  Then did I march with Surrey's power,
  What time we razed old Ayton Tower."

XIX

"For such-like need, my lord, I trow,
  Norham can find you guides enow;
  For here be some have pricked as far,
  On Scottish ground, as to Dunbar;
  Have drunk the monks of St. Bothan's ale,
  And driven the beeves of Lauderdale;
  Harried the wives of Greenlaw's goods,
  And given them light to set their hoods."

XX

"Now, in good sooth," Lord Marmion cried,
"Were I in warlike wise to ride,
  A better guard I would not lack
  Than your stout forayers at my back;
  But as in form of peace I go,
  A friendly messenger, to know
  Why through all Scotland, near and far,
  Their King is mustering troops for war.
  The sight of plundering Border spears

Might justify suspicious fears,
And deadly feud, or thirst of spoil,
Break out in some unseemly broil:
A herald were my fitting guide;
Or friar, sworn in peace to bide
Or pardoner, or travelling priest,
Or strolling pilgrim, at the least."

XXI

The captain mused a little space,
And passed his hand across his face.
"Fain would I find the guide you want,
But ill may pursuivant,
The only men that safe can ride
Mine errands on the Scottish side:
And though a bishop built this fort,
Few holy brethren here resort;
Even our good chaplain, as I ween,
Since our last siege we have not seen:
The mass he might not sing or say,
Upon one stinted meal a day;
So safe he sat in Durham aisle,
And prayed for our success the while.
Our Norham vicar, woe betide,
Is all too well in case to ride;
The priest of Shoreswood—he could rein
The wildest war-horse in your train;
But then, no spearman in the hall
Will sooner swear, or stab, or brawl.
Friar John of Tillmouth were the man:
A blithesome brother at the can,
A welcome guest in hall and bower,
He knows each castle, town, and tower,
In which the wine and ale is good,
'Twixt Newcastle and Holyrood.
But that good man, as ill befalls,
Hath seldom left our castle walls,
Since, on the vigil of Saint Bede,

In evil hour, he crossed the Tweed,
To teach Dame Alison her creed.
Old Bughtrig found him with his wife;
And John, an enemy to strife,
Sans frock and hood, fled for his life.
The jealous churl hath deeply swore
That if again he venture o'er,
He shall shrive penitent no more.
Little he loves such risks, I know;
Yet in your guard, perchance, will go."

XXII

Young Selby, at the fair hall-board,
Carved to his uncle and that lord,
And reverently took up the word.
"Kind uncle, woe were we each one,
If harm should hap to brother John.
He is a man of mirthful speech,
Can many a game and gambol teach;
Full well at tables can he play,
And sweep at bowls the stake away.
None can a lustier carol bawl;
The needfullest among us all,
When time hangs heavy in the hall,
And snow comes thick at Christmas-tide,
And we can neither hunt, nor ride
A foray on the Scottish side.
The vowed revenge of Bughtrig rude,
May end in worse than loss of hood.
Let Friar John, in safety, still
In chimney-corner snore his fill,
Roast hissing crabs, or flagons swill:
Last night to Norham there came one,
Will better guide Lord Marmion."
"Nephew," quoth Heron, "by my fay,
Well hast thou spoke; say forth thy say."

XXIII

"Here is a holy Palmer come
From Salem first, and last from Rome:
One that hath kissed the blessèd tomb,
And visited each holy shrine
In Araby and Palestine;
On hills of Armenie hath been,
Where Noah's ark may yet be seen;
By that Red Sea, too, hath he trod,
Which parted at the prophet's rod;
In Sinai's wilderness he saw
The Mount where Israel heard the law,
Mid thunder-dint and flashing levin,
And shadows, mists, and darkness, given.
He shows Saint James's cockle-shell;
Of fair Montserrat, too, can tell;
    And of that grot where olives nod,
Where, darling of each heart and eye,
From all the youth of Sicily,
    Saint Rosalie retired to God.

XXIV

"To stout Saint George of Norwich merry,
Saint Thomas, too, of Canterbury,
Cuthbert of Durham, and Saint Bede,
For his sins' pardon hath he prayed.
He knows the passes of the North,
And seeks far shrines beyond the Forth;
Little he eats, and long will wake,
And drinks but of the stream or lake.
This were a guide o'er moor and dale
But when our John hath quaffed his ale,
As little as the wind that blows,
And warms itself against his nose,
Kens he, or cares, which way he goes."

XXV

"Gramercy!" quoth Lord Marmion,
"Full loth were I that Friar John,
That venerable man, for me
Were placed in fear or jeopardy.
If this same Palmer will me lead
    From hence to Holyrood,
Like his good saint I'll pay his meed,
Instead of cockle-shell or bead
    With angels fair and good.
I love such holy ramblers; still
They know to charm a weary hill,
    With song, romance, or lay:
Some jovial tale, or glee, or jest,
Some lying legend, at the least,
    They bring to cheer the way."

XXVI

"Ah! noble sir," young Selby said,
And finger on his lip he laid,
"This man knows much—perchance e'en more
Than he could learn by holy lore.
Still to himself he's muttering,
And shrinks as at some unseen thing.
Last night we listened at his cell;
Strange sounds we heard, and, sooth to tell,
He murmured on till morn, howe'er
No living mortal could be near.
Sometimes I thought I heard it plain,
As other voices spoke again.
I cannot tell—I like it not—
Friar John hath told us it is wrote,
No conscience clear, and void of wrong,
Can rest awake, and pray so long.
Himself still sleeps before his beads
Have marked ten aves, and two creeds."

XXVII

"Let pass," quoth Marmion; "by my fay,
This man shall guide me on my way,
Although the great arch-fiend and he
Had sworn themselves of company.
So please you, gentle youth, to call
This Palmer to the castle-hall."
The summoned Palmer came in place;
His sable cowl o'erhung his face;
In his black mantle was he clad,
With Peter's keys, in cloth of red,
    On his broad shoulders wrought;
The scallop-shell his cap did deck;
The crucifix around his neck
    Was from Loretto brought;
His sandals were with travel tore,
Staff, budget, bottle, scrip, he wore;
The faded palm-branch in his hand
Showed pilgrim from the Holy Land.

XXVIII

Whenas the Palmer came in hall,
Nor lord, nor knight, was there more tall,
    Or had a statelier step withal,
Or looked more high and keen;
For no saluting did he wait,
But strode across the hall of state,
And fronted Marmion where he sate,
    As he his peer had been.
But his gaunt frame was worn with toil;
His cheek was sunk, alas, the while!
And when he struggled at a smile
    His eye looked haggard wild:
Poor wretch! the mother that him bare,
If she had been in presence there,
In his wan face and sun-burned hair,
    She had not known her child.

Danger, long travel, want, or woe,
Soon change the form that best we know—
For deadly fear can time outgo,
 And blanch at once the hair;
Hard toil can roughen form and face,
And want can quench the eye's bright grace,
Nor does old age a wrinkle trace
 More deeply than despair.
Happy whom none of these befall,
But this poor Palmer knew them all.

XXIX

Lord Marmion then his boon did ask;
The Palmer took on him the task,
So he would march with morning tide,
To Scottish court to be his guide.
"But I have solemn vows to pay,
And may not linger by the way,
 To fair St. Andrews bound,
Within the ocean-cave to pray,
Where good Saint Rule his holy lay,
From midnight to the dawn of day,
 Sung to the billows' sound;
Thence to Saint Fillan's blessèd well,
Whose springs can frenzied dreams dispel,
 And the crazed brain restore:
Saint Mary grant that cave or spring
Could back to peace my bosom bring,
 Or bid it throb no more!"

XXX

And now the midnight draught of sleep,
Where wine and spices richly steep,
In massive bowl of silver deep,
 The page presents on knee.
Lord Marmion drank a fair good rest,
The captain pledged his noble guest,

The cup went through among the rest,
    Who drained it merrily;
Alone the Palmer passed it by,
Though Selby pressed him courteously.
This was a sign the feast was o'er,
It hushed the merry wassail roar,
    The minstrels ceased to sound.
Soon in the castle nought was heard
But the slow footstep of the guard,
    Pacing his sober round.

XXXI

With early dawn Lord Marmion rose:
And first the chapel doors unclose;
    Then after morning rites were done
(A hasty mass from Friar John),
And knight and squire had broke their fast
On rich substantial repast,
Lord Marmion's bugles blew to horse
Then came the stirrup-cup in course:
Between the baron and his host
No point of courtesy was lost:
High thanks were by Lord Marmion paid,
Solemn excuse the captain made,
Till, filing from the gate, had passed
That noble train, their lord the last.
Then loudly rung the trumpet call;
Thundered the cannon from the wall,
    And shook the Scottish shore:
Around the castle eddied slow,
Volumes of smoke as white as snow,
    And hid its turrets hoar;
Till they rolled forth upon the air,
And met the river breezes there,
Which gave again the prospect fair.

Introduction to Canto Second

To the Rev. John Marriott, A.M.

—Ashestiel, Ettrick Forest

THE scenes are desert now, and bare,
Where flourished once a forest fair
When these waste glens with copse were lined,
And peopled with the hart and hind.
Yon thorn—perchance whose prickly spears
Have fenced him for three hundred years,
While fell around his green compeers—
Yon lonely thorn, would he could tell
The changes of his parent dell,
Since he, so grey and stubborn now,
Waved in each breeze a sapling bough:
Would he could tell how deep the shade
A thousand mingled branches made;
How broad the shadows of the oak,
How clung the rowan to the rock,
And through the foliage showed his head,
With narrow leaves and berries red;
What pines on every mountain sprung,
O'er every dell what birches hung,
In every breeze what aspens shook,
What alders shaded every brook!

"Here, in my shade," methinks he'd say,
"The mighty stag at noontide lay:
The wolf I've seen, a fiercer game
(The neighbouring dingle bears his name),
With lurching step around me prowl,
And stop, against the moon to howl;
The mountain-boar, on battle set,
His tusks upon my stem would whet;
While doe, and roe, and red-deer good,
Have bounded by, through gay greenwood.

Then oft, from Newark's riven tower,
Sallied a Scottish monarch's power:
A thousand vassals mustered round,
With horse, and hawk, and horn, and hound;
And I might see the youth intent,
Guard every pass with crossbow bent;
And through the brake the rangers stalk,
And falc'ners hold the ready hawk;
And foresters in greenwood trim,
Lead in the leash the gazehounds grim,
Attentive as the bratchet's bay
From the dark covert drove the prey,
To slip them as he broke away.
The startled quarry bounds amain,
As fast the gallant greyhounds strain;
Whistles the arrow from the bow,
Answers the arquebuss below;
While all the rocking hills reply,
To hoof-clang, hound, and hunter's cry,
And bugles ringing lightsomely."

Of such proud huntings many tales
Yet linger in our lonely dales,
Up pathless Ettrick and on Yarrow,
Where erst the outlaw drew his arrow.
But not more blithe that silvan court,
Than we have been at humbler sport;
Though small our pomp, and mean our game
Our mirth, dear Mariott, was the same.
Remember'st thou my greyhounds true?
O'er holt or hill there never flew,
From slip or leash there never sprang,
More fleet of foot, or sure of fang.
Nor dull, between each merry chase,
Passed by the intermitted space;
For we had fair resource in store,
In Classic and in Gothic lore:
We marked each memorable scene,
And held poetic talk between;

Nor hill nor brook we paced along
But had its legend or its song.
All silent now—for now are still
Thy bowers, untenanted Bowhill!
No longer, from thy mountains dun,
The yeoman hears the well-known gun,
And while his honest heart glows Warm,
At thought of his paternal farm,
Round to his mates a brimmer fills,
And drinks, "The Chieftain of the Hills!"
No fairy forms, in Yarrow's bowers,
Trip o'er the walks, or tend the flowers,
Fair as the elves whom Janet saw
By moonlight dance on Carterhaugh;
No youthful baron's left to grace
The forest-sheriff's lonely chase,
And ape, in manly step and tone,
The majesty of Oberon:
And she is gone, whose lovely face
Is but her least and lowest grace;
Though if to sylphid queen 'twere given
To show our earth the charms of Heaven,
She could not glide along the air,
With form more light, or face more fair.
No more the widow's deafened ear
Grows quick that lady's step to hear:
At noontide she expects her not,
Nor busies her to trim the cot:
Pensive she turns her humming wheel,
Or pensive cooks her orphans' meal;
Yet blesses, ere she deals their bread,
The gentle hand by which they're fed.

From Yair,—which hills so closely bind,
Scarce can the Tweed his passage find,
Though much he fret, and chafe, and toil,
Till all his eddying currents boil,—
Her long descended lord is gone,
And left us by the stream alone.

And much I miss those sportive boys,
Companions of my mountain joys,
Just at the age 'twixt boy and youth,
When thought is speech, and speech is truth.
Close to my side, with what delight
They pressed to hear of Wallace wight,
When, pointing to his airy mound,
I called his ramparts holy ground!
Kindled their brows to hear me speak;
And I have smiled, to feel my cheek,
Despite the difference of our years,
Return again the glow of theirs.
Ah, happy boys! such feelings pure,
They will not, cannot, long endure;
Condemned to stem the world's rude tide,
You may not linger by the side;
For Fate shall thrust you from the shore,
And Passion ply the sail and oar.
Yet cherish the remembrance still,
Of the lone mountain and the rill;
For trust, dear boys, the time will come
When fiercer transport shall be dumb,
And you will think right frequently,
But, well I hope, without a sigh,
On the free hours that we have spent
Together, on the brown hill's bent.

When, musing on companions gone,
We doubly feel ourselves alone,
Something, my friend, we yet may gain;
There is a pleasure in this pain:
It soothes the love of lonely rest,
Deep in each gentler heart impressed.
'Tis silent amid worldly toils,
And stifled soon by mental broils;
But, in a bosom thus prepared,
Its still small voice is often heard,
Whispering a mingled sentiment,

'Twixt resignation and content.
Oft in my mind such thoughts awake,
By lone Saint Mary's silent lake;
Thou know'st it well,—nor fen, nor sedge,
Pollute the pure lake's crystal edge;
Abrupt and sheer, the mountains sink
At once upon the level brink;
And just a trace of silver sand
Marks where the water meets the land.
Far in the mirror, bright and blue,
Each hill's huge outline you may view;
Shaggy with heath, but lonely bare,
Nor tree, nor bush, nor brake, is there,
Save where of land yon slender line
Bears thwart the lake the scattered pine.
Yet even this nakedness has power,
And aids the feeling of the hour:
Nor thicket, dell, nor copse you spy,
Where living thing concealed might lie;
Nor point, retiring, hides a dell,
Where swain, or woodman lone, might dwell;
There's nothing left to fancy's guess,
You see that all is loneliness:
And silence aids—though the steep hills
Send to the lake a thousand rills;
In summer tide, so soft they weep,
The sound but lulls the ear asleep;
Your horse's hoof-tread sounds too rude,
So stilly is the solitude.

Nought living meets the eye or ear,
But well I ween the dead are near;
For though, in feudal strife, a foe
Hath lain our Lady's chapel low,
Yet still beneath the hallowed soil,
The peasant rests him from his toil,
And, dying, bids his bones be laid,
Where erst his simple fathers prayed.

If age had tamed the passion's strife,
And fate had cut my ties to life,
Here, have I thought, 'twere sweet to dwell
And rear again the chaplain's cell,
Like that same peaceful hermitage
Where Milton longed to spend his age.
'Twere sweet to mark the setting day
On Bourhope's lonely top decay;
And, as it faint and feeble died
On the broad lake and mountain's side,
To say, "Thus pleasures fade away;
Youth, talents, beauty, thus decay,
And leave us dark, forlorn, and grey;"
Then gaze on Dryhope's ruined tower,
And think on Yarrow's faded Flower:
And when that mountain-sound I heard,
Which bids us be for storm prepared,
The distant rustling of his wings,
As up his force the tempest brings,
'Twere sweet, ere yet his terrors rave,
To sit upon the wizard's grave—
That wizard-priest's, whose bones are thrust
From company of holy dust;
On which no sunbeam ever shines—
So superstition's creed divines—
Thence view the lake, with sullen roar,
Heave her broad billows to the shore;
And mark the wild swans mount the gale,
Spread wide through mist their snowy sail,
And ever stoop again, to lave
Their bosoms on the surging wave:
Then, when against the driving hail
No longer might my plaid avail,
Back to my lonely home retire,
And light my lamp, and trim my fire;
There ponder o'er some mystic lay,
Till the wild tale had all its sway,
And, in the bittern's distant shriek,
I heard unearthly voices speak,

And thought the wizard-priest was come
To claim again his ancient home!
And bade my busy fancy range,
To frame him fitting shape and strange,
Till from the task my brow I cleared,
And smiled to think that I had feared.

But chief 'twere sweet to think such life
(Though but escape from fortune's strife),
Something most matchless good and wise,
A great and grateful sacrifice;
And deem each hour to musing given
A step upon the road to heaven.

Yet him whose heart is ill at ease
Such peaceful solitudes displease;
He loves to drown his bosom's jar
Amid the elemental war:
And my black Palmer's choice had been
Some ruder and more savage scene,
Like that which frowns round dark Lochskene.
There eagles scream from isle to shore;
Down all the rocks the torrents roar;
O'er the black waves incessant driven,
Dark mists infect the summer heaven;
Through the rude barriers of the lake
Away its hurrying waters break,
Faster and whiter dash and curl,
Till down yon dark abyss they hurl.
Rises the fog-smoke white as snow,
Thunders the viewless stream below.
Diving, as if condemned to lave
Some demon's subterranean cave,
Who, prisoned by enchanter's spell,
Shakes the dark rock with groan and yell.
And well that Palmer's form and mien
Had suited with the stormy scene,
Just on the edge, straining his ken
To view the bottom of the den,

Where, deep deep down, and far within,
Toils with the rocks the roaring linn;
Then, issuing forth one foamy wave,
And wheeling round the giant's grave,
White as the snowy charger's tail
Drives down the pass of Moffatdale.

Marriott, thy harp, on Isis strung,
To many a Border theme has rung;
Then list to me, and thou shalt know
Of this mysterious man of woe.

Canto Second

THE CONVENT

I

THE breeze, which swept away the smoke,
 Round Norham Castle rolled,
When all the loud artillery spoke,
With lightning-flash, and thunder-stroke,
 As Marmion left the hold.
It curled not Tweed alone, that breeze,
For, far upon Northumbrian seas,
It freshly blew, and strong,
Where, from high Whitby's cloistered pile,
Bound to St. Cuthbert's holy isle,
 It bore a barque along.
Upon the gale she stooped her side,
And bounded o'er the swelling tide,
 As she were dancing home;
The merry seamen laughed to see
Their gallant ship so lustily
 Furrow the green sea-foam.
Much joyed they in their honoured freight;
For, on the deck, in chair of state,
The Abbess of Saint Hilda placed,
With five fair nuns, the galley graced.

II

'Twas sweet to see these holy maids,
Like birds escaped to greenwood shades,
 Their first flight from the cage,
How timid, and how curious too,
For all to them was strange and new,
And all the common sights they view,
 Their wonderment engage.

One eyed the shrouds and swelling sail,
With many a benedicite;
One at the rippling surge grew pale,
 And would for terror pray;
Then shrieked, because the sea-dog, nigh,
His round black head, and sparkling eye,
 Reared o'er the foaming spray;
And one would still adjust her veil,
Disordered by the summer gale,
Perchance lest some more worldly eye
Her dedicated charms might spy;
Perchance, because such action graced
Her fair-turned arm and slender waist.
Light was each simple bosom there,
Save two, who ill might pleasure share—
The Abbess and the novice Clare.

III

The Abbess was of noble blood,
But early took the veil and hood,
Ere upon life she cast a look,
Or knew the world that she forsook.
Fair too she was, and kind had been
As she was fair, but ne'er had seen
For her a timid lover sigh,
Nor knew the influence of her eye.
Love, to her ear, was but a name,
Combined with vanity and shame;
Her hopes, her fears, her joys, were all
Bounded within the cloister wall:
The deadliest sin her mind could reach
Was of monastic rule the breach;
And her ambition's highest aim
To emulate Saint Hilda's fame.
For this she gave her ample dower,
To raise the convent's eastern tower;
For this, with carving rare and quaint,
She decked the chapel of the saint,

And gave the relic-shrine of cost,
With ivory and gems embossed.
The poor her convent's bounty blest,
The pilgrim in its halls found rest.

IV

Black was her garb, her rigid rule
Reformed on Benedictine school;
Her cheek was pale, her form was spare;
Vigils, and penitence austere,
Had early quenched the light of youth,
But gentle was the dame, in sooth:
Though, vain of her religious sway,
She loved to see her maids obey;
Yet nothing stern was she in cell,
And the nuns loved their Abbess well.
Sad was this voyage to the dame;
Summoned to Lindisfarne, she came,
There, with Saint Cuthbert's Abbot old,
And Tynemouth's Prioress, to hold
A chapter of Saint Benedict,
For inquisition stern and strict,
On two apostates from the faith,
And, if need were, to doom to death.

V

Nought say I here of Sister Clare,
Save this, that she was young and fair;
As yet a novice unprofessed,
Lovely and gentle, but distressed.
She was betrothed to one now dead,
Or worse, who had dishonoured fled.
Her kinsmen bade her give her hand
To one who loved her for her land;
Herself, almost heart-broken now,
Was bent to take the vestal vow,

And shroud, within Saint Hilda's gloom,
Her blasted hopes and withered bloom.

VI

She sate upon the galley's prow,
And seemed to mark the waves below;
Nay, seemed, so fixed her look and eye,
To count them as they glided by.
She saw them not—'twas seeming all—
Far other scene her thoughts recall—
A sun-scorched desert, waste and bare,
Nor waves nor breezes murmured there;
There saw she, where some careless hand
O'er a dead corpse had heaped the sand,
To hide it till the jackals come,
To tear it from the scanty tomb.
See what a woful look was given,
As she raised up her eyes to heaven!

VII

Lovely, and gentle, and distressed—
These charms might tame the fiercest breast;
Harpers have sung, and poets told,
That he, in fury uncontrolled,
The shaggy monarch of the wood,
Before a virgin, fair and good,
Hath pacified his savage mood.
But passions in the human frame
Oft put the lion's rage to shame:
And jealousy, by dark intrigue,
With sordid avarice in league,
Had practised with their bowl and knife
Against the mourner's harmless life.
This crime was charged 'gainst those who lay
Prisoned in Cuthbert's islet grey.

VIII

And now the vessel skirts the strand
Of mountainous Northumberland;
Towns, towers, and halls successive rise,
And catch the nuns' delighted eyes.
Monkwearmouth soon behind them lay,
And Tynemouth's priory and bay;
They marked, amid her trees, the hall
Of lofty Seaton-Delaval;
They saw the Blythe and Wansbeck floods
Rush to the sea through sounding woods;
They passed the tower of Widderington,
Mother of many a valiant son;
At Coquet Isle their beads they tell
To the good saint who owned the cell;
Then did the Alne attention claim,
And Warkworth, proud of Percy's name;
And next, they crossed themselves, to hear
The whitening breakers sound so near,
Where, boiling through the rocks, they roar
On Dunstanborough's caverned shore;
Thy tower, proud Bamborough, marked they there,
King Ida's castle, huge and square,
From its tall rock look grimly down,
And on the swelling ocean frown;
Then from the coast they bore away,
And reached the Holy Island's bay.

IX

The tide did now its floodmark gain,
And girdled in the saint's domain:
For, with the flow and ebb, its style
Varies from continent to isle;
Dry-shod, o'er sands, twice every day,
The pilgrims to the shrine find way;
Twice every day, the waves efface

Of staves and sandalled feet the trace.
As to the port the galley flew,
Higher and higher rose to view
The castle with its battled walls,
The ancient monastery's halls,
A solemn, huge, and dark-red pile,
Placed on the margin of the isle.

X

In Saxon strength that abbey frowned,
With massive arches broad and round,
    That rose alternate, row and row,
     On ponderous columns, short and low,
      Built ere the art was known,
     By pointed aisle, and shafted stalk,
     The arcades of an alleyed walk
      To emulate in stone.
On the deep walls the heathen Dane
Had poured his impious rage in vain;
And needful was such strength to these,
Exposed to the tempestuous seas,
Scourged by the winds' eternal sway,
Open to rovers fierce as they,
Which could twelve hundred years withstand
Winds, waves, and northern pirates' hand.
Not but that portions of the pile,
Rebuilded in a later style,
Showed where the spoiler's hand had been;
Not hut the wasting sea-breeze keen
Had worn the pillar's carving quaint,
And mouldered in his niche the saint,
And rounded, with consuming power,
The pointed angles of each tower;
Yet still entire the abbey stood,
Like veteran, worn, but unsubdued.

Soon as they neared his turrets strong,
The maidens raised Saint Hilda's song,
 And with the sea-wave and the wind,
 Their voices, sweetly shrill, combined
  And made harmonious close;
 Then, answering from the sandy shore,
 Half-drowned amid the breakers' roar,
  According chorus rose:
 Down to the haven of the isle
 The monks and nuns in order file,
 From Cuthbert's cloisters grim;
Banner, and cross, and relics there,
To meet Saint Hilda's maids, they bare;
And, as they caught the sounds on air,
 They echoed back the hymn.
The islanders, in joyous mood,
Rushed emulously through the flood,
 To hale the barque to land;
Conspicuous by her veil and hood,
Signing the cross, the Abbess stood,
And blessed them with her hand.

Suppose we now the welcome said,
Suppose the convent banquet made:
 All through the holy dome,
Through cloister, aisle, and gallery,
Wherever vestal maid might pry,
Nor risk to meet unhallowed eye,
 The stranger sisters roam;
Till fell the evening damp with dew,
And the sharp sea-breeze coldly blew,
For there e'en summer night is chill.
Then, having strayed and gazed their fill,
 They closed around the fire;

And all, in turn, essayed to paint
The rival merits of their saint,
 A theme that ne'er can tire
A holy maid; for, be it known,
That their saint's honour is their own.

XIII

Then Whitby's nuns exulting told,
How to their house three barons bold
 Must menial service do;
While horns blow out a note of shame,
And monks cry, "Fye upon your name!
In wrath, for loss of silvan game,
 Saint Hilda's priest ye slew."
"This, on Ascension Day, each year,
While labouring on our harbour-pier,
 Must Herbert, Bruce, and Percy hear."
They told, how in their convent cell
A Saxon princess once did dwell,
 The lovely Edelfled.
And how, of thousand snakes, each one
Was changed into a coil of stone
 When holy Hilda prayed;
Themselves, within their holy bound,
Their stony folds had often found.
They told, how sea-fowls' pinions fail,
As over Whitby's towers they sail,
And, sinking down, with flutterings faint,
They do their homage to the saint.

XIV

Nor did Saint Cuthbert's daughters fail
To vie with these in holy tale;
His body's resting-place of old,
How oft their patron changed, they told;
How, when the rude Dane burned their pile,
The monks fled forth from Holy Isle;

O'er northern mountain, marsh, and moor,
From sea to sea, from shore to shore,
Seven years Saint Cuthbert's corpse they bore.
    They rested them in fair Melrose;
        But though alive he loved it well,
    Not there his relics might repose;
        For, wondrous tale to tell!
    In his stone coffin forth he rides,
    A ponderous barque for river tides,
    Yet light as gossamer it glides,
        Downward to Tilmouth cell.
Nor long was his abiding there,
For southward did the saint repair;
Chester-le-Street, and Rippon, saw
His holy corpse, ere Wardilaw
    Hailed him with joy and fear;
And, after many wanderings past,
He chose his lordly seat at last,
Where his cathedral, huge and vast,
    Looks down upon the Wear:
There, deep in Durham's Gothic shade,
His relics are in secret laid;
    But none may know the place,
Save of his holiest servants three,
Deep sworn to solemn secrecy,
    Who share that wondrous grace.

XV

Who may his miracles declare!
Even Scotland's dauntless king and heir,
    Although with them they led
Galwegians, wild as ocean's gale,
And Lodon's knights, all sheathed in mail,
And the bold men of Teviotdale,
    Before his standard fled.
'Twas he, to vindicate his reign,
Edged Alfred's falchion on the Dane,
And turned the Conqueror back again,

When, with his Norman bowyer band,
He came to waste Northumberland.

XVI

But fain Saint Hilda's nuns would learn
If, on a rock, by Lindisfarne,
Saint Cuthbert sits, and toils to frame
The sea-born beads that bear his name:
Such tales had Whitby's fishers told,
And said they might his shape behold,
 And hear his anvil sound:
A deadened clang—a huge dim form,
Seen but, and heard, when gathering storm
 And night were closing round.
But this, as tale of idle fame,
The nuns of Lindisfarne disclaim.

XVII

While round the fire such legends go,
Far different was the scene of woe,
Where, in a secret aisle beneath,
Council was held of life and death.
 It was more dark and lone, that vault,
  Than the worse dungeon cell:
 Old Colwulf built it, for his fault,
  In penitence to dwell,
When he, for cowl and beads, laid down
The Saxon battle-axe and crown.
This den, which, chilling every sense
 Of feeling, hearing, sight,
Was called the Vault of Penitence,
 Excluding air and light,
Was, by the prelate Sexhelm, made
A place of burial for such dead
As, having died in mortal sin,
Might not be laid the church within.
'Twas now a place of punishment;

Whence if so loud a shriek were sent,
    As reached the upper air,
The hearers blessed themselves, and said,
The spirits of the sinful dead
    Bemoaned their torments there.

XVIII

But though, in the monastic pile,
Did of this penitential aisle
    Some vague tradition go,
Few only, save the Abbot, knew
Where the place lay; and still more few
Were those, who had from him the clue
    To that dread vault to go.
Victim and executioner
Were blindfold when transported there.
In low dark rounds the arches hung,
From the rude rock the side-walls sprung;
The grave-stones, rudely sculptured o'er,
Half sunk in earth, by time half wore,
Were all the pavement of the floor;
The mildew-drops fell one by one,
With tinkling plash upon the stone.
A cresset, in an iron chain,
Which served to light this drear domain,
With damp and darkness seemed to strive,
As if it scarce might keep alive;
And yet it dimly served to show
The awful conclave met below.

XIX

There, met to doom in secrecy,
Were placed the heads of convents three;
All servants of Saint Benedict,
The statutes of whose order strict
    On iron table lay;
In long black dress, on seats of stone,

Behind were these three judges shown
    By the pale cresset's ray,
The Abbess of Saint Hilda's, there,
Sat for a space with visage bare,
Until, to hide her bosom's swell,
And tear-drops that for pity fell,
She closely drew her veil:
Yon shrouded figure, as I guess,
By her proud mien and flowing dress,
Is Tynemouth's haughty Prioress,
    And she with awe looks pale:
And he, that ancient man, whose sight
Has long been quenched by age's night,
Upon whose wrinkled brow alone
Nor ruth nor mercy's trace is shown,
    Whose look is hard and stern—
Saint Cuthbert's Abbot is his style
For sanctity called, through the isle,
    The saint of Lindisfarne.

XX

Before them stood a guilty pair;
But, though an equal fate they share,
Yet one alone deserves our care.
Her sex a page's dress belied;
The cloak and doublet, loosely tied,
Obscured her charms, but could not hide.
    Her cap down o'er her face she drew;
        And, on her doublet breast,
    She tried to hide the badge of blue,
        Lord Marmion's falcon crest.
But, at the Prioress' command,
A monk undid the silken band,
    That tied her tresses fair,
And raised the bonnet from her head,
And down her slender form they spread,
    In ringlets rich and rare.
Constance de Beverley they know,

Sister professed of Fontevraud,
Whom the church numbered with the dead
For broken vows, and convent fled.

XXI

When thus her face was given to view—
Although so pallid was her hue,
It did a ghastly contrast bear
To those bright ringlets glistering fair—
Her look composed, and steady eye,
Bespoke a matchless constancy;
And there she stood so calm and pale,
That, but her breathing did not fail,
And motion slight of eye and head,
And of her bosom, warranted
That neither sense nor pulse she lacks,
You might have thought a form of wax,
Wrought to the very life, was there;
So still she was, so pale, so fair.

XXII

Her comrade was a sordid soul,
    Such as does murder for a meed;
Who, but of fear, knows no control,
Because his conscience, seared and foul,
    Feels not the import of his deed;
One, whose brute-feeling ne'er aspires
Beyond his own more brute desires.
Such tools the Tempter ever needs,
To do the savagest of deeds;
For them no visioned terrors daunt,
Their nights no fancied spectres haunt,
One fear with them, of all most base,
The fear of death—alone finds place.
This wretch was clad in frock and cowl,
And shamed not loud to moan and howl,
His body on the floor to dash,

And crouch, like hound beneath the lash;
While his mute partner, standing near,
Waited her doom without a tear.

XXIII

Yet well the luckless wretch might shriek,
Well might her paleness terror speak!
For there were seen, in that dark wall,
Two niches, narrow, deep, and tall;
Who enters at such grisly door
Shall ne'er, I ween, find exit more.
In each a slender meal was laid,
Of roots, of water, and of bread:
By each, in Benedictine dress,
Two haggard monks stood motionless;
Who, holding high a blazing torch,
Showed the grim entrance of the porch:
Reflecting back the smoky beam,
The dark-red walls and arches gleam.
Hewn stones and cement were displayed,
And building tools in order laid.

XXIV

These executioners were chose,
As men who were with mankind foes,
And with despite and envy fired,
Into the cloister had retired;
    Or who, in desperate doubt of grace,
    Strove, by deep penance, to efface
        Of some foul crime the stain;
    For, as the vassals of her will,
    Such men the Church selected still,
    As either joyed in doing ill,
        Or thought more grace to gain,
If, in her cause, they wrestled down
Feelings their nature strove to own.

By strange device were they brought there,
They knew not how, nor knew not where.

XXV

And now that blind old Abbot rose,
    To speak the Chapter's doom
On those the wall was to enclose,
    Alive, within the tomb:
But stopped, because that woful maid,
Gathering her powers, to speak essayed.
Twice she essayed, and twice in vain;
Her accents might no utterance gain;
Nought but imperfect murmurs slip
From her convulsed and quivering lip;
'Twixt each attempt all was so still,
You seemed to hear a distant rill—
    'Twas ocean's swells and falls;
For though this vault of sin and fear
Was to the sounding surge so near,
A tempest there you scarce could hear,
    So massive were the walls.

XXVI

At length, an effort sent apart
The blood that curdled to her heart,
    And light came to her eye,
And colour dawned upon her cheek,
A hectic and a fluttered streak,
Like that left on the Cheviot peak,
    By autumn's stormy sky;
And when her silence broke at length,
Still as she spoke she gathered strength,
    And armed herself to bear.
It was a fearful sight to see
Such high resolve and constancy,
    In form so soft and fair.

XXVII

"I speak not to implore your grace,
Well know I, for one minute's space
    Successless might I sue:
Nor do I speak your prayers to gain—
For if a death of lingering pain,
To cleanse my sins, be penance vain,
    Vain are your masses too.
I listened to a traitor's tale,
I left the convent and the veil;
For three long years I bowed my pride,
A horse-boy in his train to ride;
And well my folly's meed he gave,
Who forfeited, to be his slave,
All here, and all beyond the grave.
He saw young Clara's face more fair,
He knew her of broad lands the heir,
Forgot his vows, his faith forswore,
And Constance was beloved no more.
    'Tis an old tale, and often told;
        But did my fate and wish agree,
    Ne'er had been read, in story old,
    Of maiden true betrayed for gold,
    That loved, or was avenged, like me.

XXVIII

"The king approved his favourite's aim;
In vain a rival barred his claim,
    Whose fate with Clare's was plight,
For he attaints that rival's fame
With treason's charge—and on they came,
    In mortal lists to fight.
        Their oaths are said,
        Their prayers are prayed,
        Their lances in the rest are laid,
    They meet in mortal shock;
And, hark! the throng, with thundering cry,

Shout 'Marmion! Marmion!' to the sky,
    'De Wilton to the block!'
Say ye, who preach Heaven shall decide
When in the lists two champions ride,
    Say, was Heaven's justice here?
When, loyal in his love and faith,
Wilton found overthrow or death,
    Beneath a traitor's spear?
How false the charge, how true he fell,
This guilty packet best can tell."
Then drew a packet from her breast,
Paused, gathered voice, and spoke the rest.

XXIX

"Still was false Marmion's bridal stayed:
To Whitby's convent fled the maid,
    The hated match to shun.
'Ho! shifts she thus?' King Henry cried;
'Sir Marmion, she shall be thy bride,
    If she were sworn a nun.'
One way remained—the King's command
Sent Marmion to the Scottish land:
I lingered here, and rescue planned
    For Clara and for me:
This caitiff monk, for gold, did swear,
He would to Whitby's shrine repair,
And, by his drugs, my rival fair
    A saint in heaven should be.
But ill the dastard kept his oath,
Whose cowardice has undone us both.

XXX

"And now my tongue the secret tells,
Not that remorse my bosom swells,
But to assure my soul that none
Shall ever wed with Marmion.
Had fortune my last hope betrayed,

This packet, to the King conveyed,
Had given him to the headsman's stroke,
Although my heart that instant broke.
Now, men of death, work forth your will,
For I can suffer, and be still;
And come he slow, or come he fast,
It is but Death who comes at last.

XXXI

"Yet dread me, from my living tomb,
Ye vassal slaves of bloody Rome!
If Marmion's late remorse should wake,
Full soon such vengeance will he take,
That you shall wish the fiery Dane
Had rather been your guest again.
Behind, a darker hour ascends!
The altars quake, the crosier bends,
The ire of a despotic king
Rides forth upon destruction's wing;
Then shall these vaults, so strong and deep,
Burst open to the sea-winds' sweep;
Some traveller then shall find my bones
Whitening amid disjointed stones,
And, ignorant of priests' cruelty,
Marvel such relics here should be."

XXXII

Fixed was her look, and stern her air:
Back from her shoulders streamed her hair;
The locks, that wont her brow to shade,
Stared up erectly from her head;
Her figure seemed to rise more high;
Her voice, despair's wild energy
Had given a tone of prophecy.
Appalled the astonished conclave sate:
With stupid eyes, the men of fate
Gazed on the light inspirèd form,

And listened for the avenging storm;
The judges felt the victim's dread;
No hand was moved, no word was said,
Till thus the Abbot's doom was given,
Raising his sightless balls to heaven:—
"Sister, let thy sorrows cease;
Sinful brother, part in peace!"
    From that dire dungeon, place of doom,
    Of execution too, and tomb,
        Paced forth the judges three,
    Sorrow it were, and shame, to tell
The butcher-work that there befell,
When they had glided from the cell
    Of sin and misery.

XXXIII

A hundred winding steps convey
That conclave to the upper day;
But, ere they breathed the fresher air,
They heard the shriekings of despair,
    And many a stifled groan:
With speed their upward way they take,
Such speed as age and fear can make,
And crossed themselves for terror's sake,
    As hurrying, tottering on:
Even in the vesper's heavenly tone,
They seemed to hear a dying groan,
And bade the passing knell to toll
For welfare of a parting soul.
Slow o'er the midnight wave it swung,
Northumbrian rocks in answer rung;
To Warkworth cell the echoes rolled,
His beads the wakeful hermit told,
The Bamborough peasant raised his head,
But slept ere half a prayer he said;
So far was heard the mighty knell,
The stag sprung up on Cheviot Fell,
Spread his broad nostril to the wind,

Listed before, aside, behind,
Then couched him down beside the hind,
And quaked among the mountain fern,
To hear that sound so dull and stern.

Introduction to Canto Third

To William Erskine, Esq.

—Ashestiel, Ettrick Forest

Like April morning clouds, that pass,
With varying shadow, o'er the grass,
And imitate, on field and furrow,
Life's chequered scene of joy and sorrow;
Like streamlet of the mountain North,
Now in a torrent racing forth,
Now winding slow its silver train,
And almost slumbering on the plain;
Like breezes of the Autumn day,
Whose voice inconstant dies away,
And ever swells again as fast,
When the ear deems its murmur past;
Thus various, my romantic theme
Flits, winds, or sinks, a morning dream.
Yet pleased, our eye pursues the trace
Of light and shade's inconstant race;
Pleased, views the rivulet afar,
Weaving its maze irregular;
And pleased, we listen as the breeze
Heaves its wild sigh through Autumn trees;
Then, wild as cloud, or stream, or gale,
Flow on, flow unconfined, my tale!

Need I to thee, dear Erskine, tell
I love the license all too well,
In sounds now lowly, and now strong,
To raise the desultory song?
Oft, when mid such capricious chime,
Some transient fit of lofty rhyme
To thy kind judgment seemed excuse
For many an error of the muse,
Oft hast thou said, "If, still misspent,

Thine hours to poetry are lent,
Go, and to tame thy wandering course,
Quaff from the fountain at the source;
Approach those masters, o'er whose tomb
Immortal laurels ever bloom:
Instructive of the feebler bard,
Still from the grave their voice is heard;
From them, and from the paths they showed,
Choose honoured guide and practised road:
Nor ramble on through brake and maze,
With harpers rude, of barbarous days.

"Or deem'st thou not our later time
Yields topic meet for classic rhyme?
Hast thou no elegiac verse
For Brunswick's venerable hearse?
What! not a line, a tear, a sigh,
When valour bleeds for liberty?
Oh, hero of that glorious time,
When, with unrivalled light sublime—
Though martial Austria, and though all
The might of Russia, and the Gaul,
Though banded Europe stood her foes—
The star of Brandenburg arose!
Thou couldst not live to see her beam
For ever quenched in Jena's stream.
Lamented chief!—it was not given
To thee to change the doom of Heaven,
And crush that dragon in its birth,
Predestined scourge of guilty earth.
Lamented chief!—not thine the power
To save in that presumptuous hour,
When Prussia hurried to the field,
And snatched the spear, but left the shield!
Valour and skill 'twas thine to try,
And, tried in vain, 'twas thine to die.
Ill had it seemed thy silver hair
The last, the bitterest pang to share,
For princedom reft, and scutcheons riven,

And birthrights to usurpers given;
Thy land's, thy children's wrongs to feel,
And witness woes thou couldst not heal!
On thee relenting Heaven bestows
For honoured life an honoured close;
And when revolves, in time's sure change,
The hour of Germany's revenge,
When, breathing fury for her sake,
Some new Arminius shall awake,
Her champion, ere he strike, shall come
To whet his sword on Brunswick's tomb.

    "Or of the red-cross hero teach,
Dauntless in dungeon as on breach:
Alike to him the sea, the shore,
The brand, the bridle, or the oar.
Alike to him the war that calls
Its votaries to the shattered walls,
Which the grim Turk, besmeared with blood,
Against the invincible made good;
Or that, whose thundering voice could wake
The silence of the polar lake,
When stubborn Russ, and mettled Swede,
On the warped wave their death-game played;
Or that, where vengeance and affright
Howled round the father of the fight,
Who snatched, on Alexandria's sand,
The conqueror's wreath with dying hand.

    "Or, if to touch such chord be thine,
Restore the ancient tragic line,
And emulate the notes that rung
From the wild harp, which silent hung
By silver Avon's holy shore,
Till twice a hundred years rolled o'er;
When she, the bold enchantress, came,
With fearless hand and heart on flame!
From the pale willow snatched the treasure,
And swept it with a kindred measure,

Till Avon's swans, while rung the grove
With Montfort's hate and Basil's love,
Awakening at the inspired strain,
Deemed their own Shakespeare lived again."

    Thy friendship thus thy judgment wronging,
With praises not to me belonging,
In task more meet for mightiest powers,
Wouldst thou engage my thriftless hours.
But say, my Erskine, hast thou weighed
That secret power by all obeyed,
Which warps not less the passive mind,
Its source concealed, or undefined:
Whether an impulse, that has birth
Soon as the infant wakes on earth,
One with our feelings and our powers,
And rather part of us than ours;
Or whether fitlier termed the sway
Of habit formed in early day?
Howe'er derived, its force confessed
Rules with despotic sway the breast,
And drags us on by viewless chain,
While taste and reason plead in vain.
Look east, and ask the Belgian why,
Beneath Batavia's sultry sky,
He seeks not eager to inhale
The freshness of the mountain gale,
Content to rear his whitened wall
Beside the dank and dull canal?
He'll say, from youth he loved to see
The white sail gliding by the tree.
Or see yon weather-beaten hind,
Whose sluggish herds before him wind,
Whose tattered plaid and rugged cheek
His northern clime and kindred speak;
Through England's laughing meads he goes,
And England's wealth around him flows;
Ask, if it would content him well,
At ease in those gay plains to dwell,

Where hedgerows spread a verdant screen,
And spires and forests intervene,
And the neat cottage peeps between?
No! not for these would he exchange
His dark Lochaber's boundless range:
Nor for fair Devon's meads forsake
Ben Nevis grey, and Garry's lake.

Thus while I ape the measure wild
Of tales that charmed me yet a child,
Rude though they be, still with the chime
Return the thoughts of early time;
And feelings, roused in life's first day,
Glow in the line and prompt the lay.
Then rise those crags, that mountain tower,
Which charmed my fancy's wakening hour.
Though no broad river swept along,
To claim, perchance, heroic song;
Though sighed no groves in summer gale,
To prompt of love a softer tale;
Though scarce a puny streamlet's speed
Claimed homage from a shepherd's reed;
Yet was poetic impulse given,
By the green hill and clear blue heaven.
It was a barren scene, and wild,
Where naked cliffs were rudely piled;
But ever and anon between
Lay velvet tufts of loveliest green;
And well the lonely infant knew
Recesses where the wallflower grew,
And honeysuckle loved to crawl
Up the low crag and ruined wall.
I deemed such nooks the sweetest shade
The sun in all its round surveyed;
And still I thought that shattered tower
The mightiest work of human power;
And marvelled as the aged hind
With some strange tale bewitched my mind,
Of forayers, who, with headlong force,

Down from that strength had spurred their horse,
Their southern rapine to renew,
Far in the distant Cheviots blue,
And, home returning, filled the hall
With revel, wassail-rout, and brawl.
Methought that still, with trump and clang,
The gateway's broken arches rang;
Methought grim features, seamed with scars,
Glared through the window's rusty bars,
And ever, by the winter hearth,
Old tales I heard of woe or mirth,
Of lovers' slights, of ladies' charms,
Of witches' spells, of warriors' arms;
Of patriot battles, won of old
By Wallace wight and Bruce the bold;
Of later fields of feud and fight,
When, pouring from their Highland height,
The Scottish clans, in headlong sway,
Had swept the scarlet ranks away.
While stretched at length upon the floor,
Again I fought each combat o'er,
Pebbles and shells, in order laid,
The mimic ranks of war displayed;
And onward still the Scottish Lion bore,
And still the scattered Southron fled before.

Still, with vain fondness, could I trace,
Anew, each kind familiar face,
That brightened at our evening fire!
From the thatched mansion's grey-haired sire,
Wise without learning, plain and good,
And sprung of Scotland's gentler blood;
Whose eye, in age, quick, clear, and keen,
Showed what in youth its glance had been;
Whose doom discording neighbours sought,
Content with equity unbought;
To him the venerable priest,
Our frequent and familiar guest,
Whose life and manners well could paint

Alike the student and the saint;
Alas! whose speech too oft I broke
With gambol rude and timeless joke:
For I was wayward, bold, and wild,
A self-willed imp, a grandame's child;
But, half a plague, and half a jest,
Was still endured, beloved, caressed.

    For me, thus nurtured, dost thou ask
The classic poet's well-conned task?
Nay, Erskine, nay—On the wild hill
Let the wild heathbell flourish still;
Cherish the tulip, prune the vine,
But freely let the woodbine twine,
And leave untrimmed the eglantine:
Nay, my friend, nay—Since oft thy praise
Hath given fresh vigour to my lays;
Since oft thy judgment could refine
My flattened thought, or cumbrous line;
Still kind, as is thy wont, attend,
And in the minstrel spare the friend.
Though wild as cloud, as stream, as gale,
Flow forth, flow unrestrained, my tale!

Canto Third

THE INN

I

The livelong day Lord Marmion rode:
The mountain path the Palmer showed,
By glen and streamlet winded still,
Where stunted birches hid the rill.
They might not choose the lowland road,
For the Merse forayers were abroad,
Who, fired with hate and thirst of prey,
Had scarcely failed to bar their way.
Oft on the trampling band, from crown
Of some tall cliff, the deer looked down;
On wing of jet, from his repose
In the deep heath, the blackcock rose;
Sprung from the gorse the timid roe,
Nor waited for the bending bow;
And when the stony path began,
By which the naked peak they wan,
Up flew the snowy ptarmigan.
The noon had long been passed before
They gained the height of Lammermoor;
Thence winding down the northern way,
Before them, at the close of day,
Old Gifford's towers and hamlet lay.

II

No summons calls them to the tower,
To spend the hospitable hour.
To Scotland's camp the lord was gone;
His cautious dame, in bower alone,
Dreaded her castle to unclose,
So late, to unknown friends or foes,

On through the hamlet as they paced,
Before a porch, whose front was graced
With bush and flagon trimly placed,
    Lord Marmion drew his rein:
The village inn seemed large, though rude:
Its cheerful fire and hearty food
    Might well relieve his train.
Down from their seats the horsemen sprung,
With jingling spurs the courtyard rung;
They bind their horses to the stall,
For forage, food, and firing call,
And various clamour fills the hall:
Weighing the labour with the cost,
Toils everywhere the bustling host.

III

Soon by the chimney's merry blaze,
Through the rude hostel might you gaze;
Might see, where, in dark nook aloof,
The rafters of the sooty roof
    Bore wealth of winter cheer;
Of sea-fowl dried, and solands store
And gammons of the tusky boar,
    And savoury haunch of deer.
The chimney arch projected wide;
Above, around it, and beside,
    Were tools for housewives' hand;
Nor wanted, in that martial day,
The implements of Scottish fray,
    The buckler, lance, and brand.
Beneath its shade, the place of state,
On oaken settle Marmion sate,
And viewed around the blazing hearth
His followers mix in noisy mirth;
Whom with brown ale, in jolly tide,
From ancient vessels ranged aside,
Full actively their host supplied.

IV

Theirs was the glee of martial breast,
And laughter theirs at little jest;
And oft Lord Marmion deigned to aid,
And mingle in the mirth they made;
For though, with men of high degree,
The proudest of the proud was he,
Yet, trained in camps, he knew the art
To win the soldier's hardy heart.
They love a captain to obey,
Boisterous as March, yet fresh as May;
With open hand, and brow as free,
Lover of wine and minstrelsy;
Ever the first to scale a tower,
As venturous in a lady's bower:
Such buxom chief shall lead his host
From India's fires to Zembla's frost.

V

Resting upon his pilgrim staff,
    Right opposite the Palmer stood;
His thin dark visage seen but half,
    Half hidden by his hood.
Still fixed on Marmion was his look,
Which he, who ill such gaze could brook,
    Strove by a frown to quell;
But not for that, though more than once
Full met their stern encountering glance,
    The Palmer's visage fell.

VI

By fits less frequent from the crowd
Was heard the burst of laughter loud
For still, as squire and archer stared
On that dark face and matted beard
    Their glee and game declined.

All gazed at length in silence drear,
Unbroke, save when in comrade's ear
Some yeoman, wondering in his fear,
  Thus whispered forth his mind:—
"Saint Mary! saw'st thou e'er such sight?
How pale his cheek, his eye how bright,
Whene'er the firebrand's fickle light
  Glances beneath his cowl!
Full on our lord he sets his eye;
For his best palfrey, would not I
Endure that sullen scowl."

VII

But Marmion, as to chase the awe
Which thus had quelled their hearts, who saw
The ever-varying firelight show
That figure stern and face of woe,
  Now called upon a squire:
"Fitz-Eustace, know'st thou not some lay,
To speed the lingering night away?
  We slumber by the fire."

VIII

"So please you," thus the youth rejoined,
"Our choicest minstrel's left behind.
Ill may we hope to please your ear,
Accustomed Constant's strains to hear.
The harp full deftly can he strike,
And wake the lover's lute alike;
To dear Saint Valentine, no thrush
Sings livelier from a spring-tide bush,
No nightingale her lovelorn tune
More sweetly warbles to the moon.
Woe to the cause, whate'er it be,
Detains from us his melody,
Lavished on rocks, and billows stern,
Or duller monks of Lindisfarne.

Now must I venture, as I may
To sing his favourite roundelay."

IX

A mellow voice Fitz-Eustace had,
The air he chose was wild and sad;
Such have I heard, in Scottish land,
Rise from the busy harvest band,
When falls before the mountaineer,
On Lowland plains, the ripened ear.
Now one shrill voice the notes prolong,
Now a wild chorus swells the song:
Oft have I listened, and stood still,
As it came softened up the hill,
And deemed it the lament of men
Who languished for their native glen;
And thought how sad would be such sound
On Susquehana's swampy ground,
Kentucky's wood-encumbered brake,
Or wild Ontario's boundless lake,
Where heart-sick exiles, in the strain,
Recalled fair Scotland's hills again!

X

Song

Where shall the lover rest,
    Whom the fates sever
From his true maiden's breast,
    Parted for ever?
Where, through groves deep and high,
    Sounds the far billow,
Where early violets die,
    Under the willow.

Eleu loro, &c. Soft shall be his pillow.
There, through the summer day,
 Cool streams are laving;
There, while the tempests sway,
 Scarce are boughs waving;
There, thy rest shalt thou take,
 Parted for ever,
Never again to wake,
 Never, oh, never!

Chorus

Eleu loro, &c. Never, oh, never!

XI

Where shall the traitor rest,
 He, the deceiver,
Who could win maiden's breast,
 Ruin, and leave her?
In the lost battle,
 Borne down by the flying,
Where mingles war's rattle
 With groans of the dying.

Chorus

Eleu loro, &c. There shall he be lying.
Her wing shall the eagle flap
 O'er the false-hearted;
His warm blood the wolf shall lap,
 Ere life be parted.
Shame and dishonour sit
 By his grave ever:
Blessing shall hallow it,
 Never, oh, never!

Eleu loro, &c. Never, oh, never!

XII

It ceased, the melancholy sound;
And silence sunk on all around.
The air was sad; but sadder still
    It fell on Marmion's ear,
And plained as if disgrace and ill,
    And shameful death, were near.
He drew his mantle past his face,
    Between it and the band,
And rested with his head a space
    Reclining on his hand.
His thoughts I scan not; but I ween,
That, could their import have been seen,
The meanest groom in all the hall,
That e'er tied courser to a stall,
Would scarce have wished to be their prey,
For Lutterward and Fontenaye.

XIII

High minds, of native pride and force,
Most deeply feel thy pangs, Remorse!
Fear, for their scourge, mean villains have,
Thou art the torturer of the brave!
Yet fatal strength they boast to steel
Their minds to bear the wounds they feel,
Even while they writhe beneath the smart
Of civil conflict in the heart.
For soon Lord Marmion raised his head,
And, smiling, to Fitz-Eustace said—
"Is it not strange, that, as ye sung,
  Seemed in mine ear a death-peal rung,
  Such as in nunneries they toll
  For some departing sister's soul;

Say, what may this portend?"
Then first the Palmer silence broke,
(The livelong day he had not spoke)
    "The death of a dear friend."

XIV

Marmion, whose steady heart and eye
Ne'er changed in worst extremity;
Marmion, whose soul could scantly brook,
Even from his king, a haughty look:
Whose accent of command controlled,
In camps, the boldest of the bold;
Thought, look, and utterance failed him now—
Fall'n was his glance, and flushed his brow:
    For either in the tone,
Or something in the Palmer's look,
So full upon his conscience strook,
    That answer he found none.
Thus oft it haps, that when within
They shrink at sense of secret sin,
    A feather daunts the brave;
A fool's wild speech confounds the wise,
And proudest princes veil their eyes
    Before their meanest slave.

XV

Well might he falter!—By his aid
Was Constance Beverley betrayed.
Not that he augured of the doom,
Which on the living closed the tomb:
But, tired to hear the desperate maid
Threaten by turns, beseech, upbraid;
And wroth, because in wild despair
She practised on the life of Clare;
Its fugitive the Church he gave,
Though not a victim, but a slave;
And deemed restraint in convent strange

Would hide her wrongs, and her revenge.
Himself, proud Henry's favourite peer,
Held Romish thunders idle fear;
Secure his pardon he might hold,
For some slight mulct of penance-gold.
Thus judging, he gave secret way,
When the stern priests surprised their prey.
His train but deemed the favourite page
Was left behind, to spare his age
Or other if they deemed, none dared
To mutter what he thought and heard;
Woe to the vassal, who durst pry
Into Lord Marmion's privacy!

XVI

His conscience slept, he deemed her well,
And safe secured in distant cell;
But, wakened by her favourite lay,
And that strange Palmer's boding say,
That fell so ominous and drear
Full on the object of his fear,
To aid remorse's venomed throes
Dark tales of convent-vengeance rose;
And Constance, late betrayed and scorned,
All lovely on his soul returned;
Lovely as when, at treacherous call,
She left her convent's peaceful wall,
Crimsoned with shame, with terror mute,
Dreading alike, escape, pursuit,
Till love, victorious o'er alarms,
Hid fears and blushes in his arms.

XVII

"Alas!" he thought, "how changed that mien!
How changed these timid looks have been,
Since years of guilt and of disguise
Have steeled her brow, and armed her eyes!

No more of virgin terror speaks
The blood that mantles in her cheeks:
Fierce and unfeminine, are there,
Frenzy for joy, for grief despair:
And I the cause—for whom were given
Her peace on earth, her hopes in heaven!
Would," thought he, as the picture grows,
"I on its stalk had left the rose!
Oh, why should man's success remove
The very charms that wake his love!
Her convent's peaceful solitude
Is now a prison harsh and rude;
And, pent within the narrow cell,
How will her spirit chafe and swell!
How brook the stern monastic laws!
The penance how—and I the cause!
Vigil and scourge—perchance even worse!"
And twice he rose to cry, "To horse!"
And twice his sovereign's mandate came,
Like damp upon a kindling flame;
And twice he thought, "Gave I not charge
She should be safe, though not at large?
They durst not, for their island, shred
One golden ringlet from her head."

XVIII

While thus in Marmion's bosom strove
Repentance and reviving love,
Like whirlwinds, whose contending sway
I've seen Loch Vennachar obey,
Their host the Palmer's speech had heard,
And, talkative, took up the word:
    "Ay, reverend Pilgrim, you, who stray
From Scotland's simple land away,
    To visit realms afar,
Full often learn the art to know
Of future weal, or future woe,
    By word, or sign, or star;

Yet might a knight his fortune hear,
If, knightlike, he despises fear,
Not far from hence; if fathers old
Aright our hamlet legend told."
These broken words the menials move,
For marvels still the vulgar love,
And, Marmion giving license cold,
His tale the host thus gladly told:

XIX

The Host's Tale

"A clerk could tell what years have flown
Since Alexander filled our throne,
Third monarch of that warlike name,
And eke the time when here he came
To seek Sir Hugo, then our lord;
A braver never drew a sword;
A wiser never, at the hour
Of midnight, spoke the word of power:
The same, whom ancient records call
The founder of the Goblin Hall.
I would, Sir Knight, your longer stay
Gave you that cavern to survey.
Of lofty roof, and ample size,
Beneath the castle deep it lies:
To hew the living rock profound,
The floor to pave, the arch to round,
There never toiled a mortal arm—
It all was wrought by word and charm;
And I have heard my grandsire say,
That the wild clamour and affray
Of those dread artisans of hell,
Who laboured under Hugo's spell,
Sounded as loud as ocean's war
Among the caverns of Dunbar.

XX

"The king Lord Gifford's castle sought,
  Deep labouring with uncertain thought:
  Even then he mustered all his host,
  To meet upon the western coast:
  For Norse and Danish galleys plied
  Their oars within the frith of Clyde.
  There floated Haco's banner trim,
  Above Norwayan warriors grim,
  Savage of heart, and large of limb;
  Threatening both continent and isle,
  Bute, Arran, Cunninghame, and Kyle.
  Lord Gifford, deep beneath the ground,
  Heard Alexander's bugle sound,
  And tarried not his garb to change,
  But, in his wizard habit strange,
  Came forth—a quaint and fearful sight:
  His mantle lined with fox-skins white;
  His high and wrinkled forehead bore
  A pointed cap, such as of yore
  Clerks say that Pharaoh's Magi wore:
  His shoes were marked with cross and spell,
  Upon his breast a pentacle;
  His zone, of virgin parchment thin,
  Or, as some tell, of dead man's skin,
  Bore many a planetary sign,
  Combust, and retrograde, and trine;
  And in his hand he held prepared
  A naked sword without a guard.

XXI

"Dire dealings with the fiendish race
  Had marked strange lines upon his face:
  Vigil and fast had worn him grim,
  His eyesight dazzled seemed and dim,
  As one unused to upper day;
  Even his own menials with dismay

Beheld, Sir Knight, the grisly sire,
In his unwonted wild attire;
Unwonted, for traditions run,
He seldom thus beheld the sun.
'I know,' he said—his voice was hoarse,
And broken seemed its hollow force—
'I know the cause, although untold,
Why the king seeks his vassal's hold:
Vainly from me my liege would know
His kingdom's future weal or woe
But yet, if strong his arm and heart,
His courage may do more than art.

XXII

'"Of middle air the demons proud,
Who ride upon the racking cloud,
Can read, in fixed or wandering star,
The issues of events afar;
But still their sullen aid withhold,
Save when by mightier force controlled.
Such late I summoned to my hall;
And though so potent was the call,
That scarce the deepest nook of hell
I deemed a refuge from the spell,
Yet, obstinate in silence still,
The haughty demon mocks my skill.
But thou—who little know'st thy might,
As born upon that blessèd night
When yawning graves, and dying groan,
Proclaimed hell's empire overthrown—
With untaught valour shalt compel
Response denied to magic spell.'
'Gramercy,' quoth our monarch free,
    Place him but front to front with me,
And by this good and honoured brand,
The gift of Coeur-de-Lion's hand,
Soothly I swear, that, tide what tide,
The demon shall a buffet bide.'

His bearing bold the wizard viewed,
And thus, well pleased, his speech renewed:
'There spoke the blood of Malcolm!—mark:
Forth pacing hence, at midnight dark,
The rampart seek, whose circling crown
Crests the ascent of yonder down:
A southern entrance shalt thou find;
There halt, and there thy bugle wind,
And trust thine elfin foe to see,
In guise of thy worst enemy:
Couch then thy lance, and spur thy steed—
Upon him! and Saint George to speed!
If he go down, thou soon shalt know
Whate'er these airy sprites can show;
If thy heart fail thee in the strife,
I am no warrant for thy life.'

XXIII

"Soon as the midnight bell did ring,
Alone, and armed, forth rode the king
To that old camp's deserted round:
Sir Knight, you well might mark the mound
Left-hand the town—the Pictish race,
The trench, long since, in blood did trace:
The moor around is brown and bare,
The space within is green and fair.
The spot our village children know,
For there the earliest wildflowers grow;
But woe betide the wandering wight
That treads its circle in the night!
The breadth across, a bowshot clear,
Gives ample space for full career:
Opposed to the four points of heaven,
By four deep gaps are entrance given.
The southernmost our monarch passed,
Halted, and blew a gallant blast;
And on the north, within the ring,
Appeared the form of England's king

Who then, a thousand leagues afar,
In Palestine waged holy war:
Yet arms like England's did he wield,
Alike the leopards in the shield,
Alike his Syrian courser's frame,
The rider's length of limb the same:
Long afterwards did Scotland know,
Fell Edward was her deadliest foe.

XXIV

"The vision made our monarch start,
But soon he manned his noble heart,
And in the first career they ran,
The Elfin Knight fell, horse and man;
Yet did a splinter of his lance
Through Alexander's visor glance,
And razed the skin—a puny wound.
The King, light leaping to the ground,
With naked blade his phantom foe
Compelled the future war to show.
Of Largs he saw the glorious plain,
Where still gigantic bones remain,
    Memorial of the Danish war;
Himself he saw, amid the field,
On high his brandished war-axe wield,
    And strike proud Haco from his car,
While all around the shadowy kings
Denmark's grim ravens cowered their wings.
'Tis said, that, in that awful night,
Remoter visions met his sight,
Foreshowing future conquests far,
When our son's sons wage northern war;
A royal city, tower and spire,
Reddened the midnight sky with fire,
And shouting crews her navy bore,
Triumphant to the victor shore.
Such signs may learned clerks explain—
They pass the wit of simple swain.

XXV

"The joyful King turned home again,
Headed his host, and quelled the Dane;
But yearly, when returned the night
Of his strange combat with the sprite,
    His wound must bleed and smart;
Lord Gifford then would gibing say,
'Bold as ye were, my liege, ye pay
    The penance of your start.'
Long since, beneath Dunfermline's nave,
King Alexander fills his grave,
    Our Lady give him rest!
Yet still the knightly spear and shield
The Elfin Warrior doth wield,
    Upon the brown hill's breast;
And many a knight hath proved his chance,
In the charmed ring to break a lance,
    But all have foully sped;
Save two, as legends tell, and they
Were Wallace wight, and Gilbert Hay.
    Gentles, my tale is said."

XXVI

The quaighs were deep, the liquors strong,
And on the tale the yeoman-throng
Had made a comment sage and long,
    But Marmion gave a sign:
And, with their lord, the squires retire;
The rest around the hostel fire,
    Their drowsy limbs recline:
For pillow, underneath each head,
The quiver and the targe were laid.
Deep slumbering on the hostel floor,
Oppressed with toil and ale, they snore:
The dying flame, in fitful change,
Threw on the group its shadows strange.

XXVII

Apart, and nestling in the hay
Of a waste loft, Fitz-Eustace lay;
Scarce by the pale moonlight, were seen
The foldings of his mantle green:
Lightly he dreamt, as youth will dream
Of sport by thicket, or by stream
Of hawk or hound, of ring or glove,
Or, lighter yet, of lady's love.
A cautious tread his slumber broke,
And close beside him, when he woke,
In moonbeam half, and half in gloom,
Stood a tall form, with nodding plume;
But ere his dagger Eustace drew,
His master Marmion's voice he knew.

XXVIII

"Fitz-Eustace! rise,—I cannot rest;—
Yon churl's wild legend haunts my breast,
And graver thoughts have chafed my mood;
The air must cool my feverish blood;
And fain would I ride forth, to see
The scene of elfin chivalry.
Arise, and saddle me my steed;
And, gentle Eustace, take good heed
Thou dost not rouse these drowsy slaves;
I would not, that the prating knaves
Had cause for saying, o'er their ale,
That I could credit such a tale."
Then softly down the steps they slid;
Eustace the stable door undid,
And darkling, Marmion's steed arrayed,
While, whispering, thus the baron said:—

XXIX

"Didst never, good my youth, hear tell,
    That on the hour when I was born,
 Saint George, who graced my sire's chapelle,
Down from his steed of marble fell,
    A weary wight forlorn?
The flattering chaplains all agree,
The champion left his steed to me.
I would, the omen's truth to show,
That I could meet this elfin foe!
Blithe would I battle, for the right
To ask one question at the sprite;—
Vain thought! for elves, if elves there be,
An empty race, by fount or sea,
To dashing waters dance and sing,
Or round the green oak wheel their ring."
Thus speaking, he his steed bestrode,
And from the hostel slowly rode.

XXX

Fitz-Eustace followed him abroad,
And marked him pace the village road,
    And listened to his horse's tramp,
    Till by the lessening sound,
    He judged that of the Pictish camp
    Lord Marmion sought the round.
Wonder it seemed, in the squire's eyes,
That one so wary held, and wise—
Of whom 'twas said, he scarce received
For gospel what the Church believed—
    Should, stirred by idle tale,
Ride forth in silence of the night,
As hoping half to meet a sprite,
    Arrayed in plate and mail.
For little did Fitz-Eustace know,
That passions, in contending flow,
    Unfix the strongest mind;

Wearied from doubt to doubt to flee,
We welcome fond credulity,
     Guide confident, though blind.

XXXI

Little for this Fitz-Eustace cared,
But, patient, waited till he heard,
At distance, pricked to utmost speed,
The foot-tramp of a flying steed,
     Come townward rushing on;
First, dead, as if on turf it trode,
Then, clattering on the village road—
In other pace than forth he yode,
     Returned Lord Marmion.
Down hastily he sprung from selle,
And, in his haste, well-nigh he fell:
To the squire's hand the rein he threw,
And spoke no word as he withdrew:
But yet the moonlight did betray
The falcon-crest was soiled with clay;
And plainly might Fitz-Eustace see,
By stains upon the charger's knee,
And his left side, that on the moor
He had not kept his footing sure.
Long musing on these wondrous signs,
At length to rest the squire reclines,
Broken and short; for still, between,
Would dreams of terror intervene:
Eustace did ne'er so blithely mark
The first notes of the morning lark.

Introduction to Canto Fourth

To James Skene, Esq.

—Ashestiel, Ettrick Forest

An ancient minstrel sagely said,
"Where is the life which late we led?"
That motley clown in Arden wood,
Whom humorous Jaques with envy viewed,
Not even that clown could amplify,
On this trite text, so long as I.
Eleven years we now may tell,
Since we have known each other well;
Since, riding side by side, our hand,
First drew the voluntary brand;
And sure, through many a varied scene,
Unkindness never came between.
Away these wingèd years have flown,
To join the mass of ages gone;
And though deep marked, like all below,
With checkered shades of joy and woe;
Though thou o'er realms and seas hast ranged,
Marked cities lost, and empires changed,
While here, at home, my narrower ken
Somewhat of manners saw, and men;
Though varying wishes, hopes, and fears,
Fevered the progress of these years,
Yet now, days, weeks, and months but seem
The recollection of a dream,
So still we glide down to the sea
Of fathomless eternity.
       Even now it scarcely seems a day,
Since first I tuned this idle lay;
A task so often thrown aside,
When leisure graver cares denied,
That now, November's dreary gale,
Whose voice inspired my opening tale,

That same November gale once more
Whirls the dry leaves on Yarrow shore.
Their vexed boughs streaming to the sky,
Once more our naked birches sigh,
And Blackhouse heights, and Ettrick Pen,
Have donned their wintry shrouds again:
And mountain dark, and flooded mead,
Bid us forsake the banks of Tweed.
Earlier than wont along the sky,
Mixed with the rack, the snow mists fly;
The shepherd, who in summer sun,
Had something of our envy won,
As thou with pencil, I with pen,
The features traced of hill and glen;—
He who, outstretched the livelong day,
At ease among the heath-flowers lay,
Viewed the light clouds with vacant look,
Or slumbered o'er his tattered book,
Or idly busied him to guide
His angle o'er the lessened tide;—
At midnight now, the snowy plain
Finds sterner labour for the swain.

    When red hath set the beamless sun,
Through heavy vapours dark and dun;
When the tired ploughman, dry and warm,
Hears, half-asleep, the rising storm
Hurling the hail, and sleeted rain,
Against the casement's tinkling pane;
The sounds that drive wild deer, and fox,
To shelter in the brake and rocks,
Are warnings which the shepherd ask
To dismal and to dangerous task.
Oft he looks forth, and hopes, in vain,
The blast may sink in mellowing rain;
Till, dark above, and white below,
Decided drives the flaky snow,
And forth the hardy swain must go.
Long, with dejected look and whine,
To leave the hearth his dogs repine;

Whistling and cheering them to aid,
Around his back he wreathes the plaid:
His flock he gathers, and he guides,
To open downs, and mountain-sides,
Where, fiercest though the tempest blow,
Least deeply lies the drift below.
The blast that whistles o'er the fells,
Stiffens his locks to icicles;
Oft he looks back, while, streaming far,
His cottage window seems a star—
Loses its feeble gleam,—and then
Turns patient to the blast again,
And, facing to the tempest's sweep,
Drives through the gloom his lagging sheep.
If fails his heart, if his limbs fail,
Benumbing death is in the gale:
His paths, his landmarks, all unknown,
Close to the hut, no more his own,
Close to the aid he sought in vain,
The morn may find the stiffened swain:
The widow sees, at dawning pale,
His orphans raise their feeble wail:
And, close beside him, in the snow,
Poor Yarrow, partner of their woe,
Couches upon his master's breast,
And licks his cheek to break his rest.

  Who envies now the shepherd's lot,
His healthy fare, his rural cot,
His summer couch by greenwood tree,
His rustic kirn's loud revelry,
His native hill-notes tuned on high,
To Marion of the blithesome eye;
His crook, his scrip, his oaten reed,
And all Arcadia's golden creed?

  Changes not so with us, my Skene,
Of human life the varying scene?
Our youthful summer oft we see
Dance by on wings of game and glee,
While the dark storm reserves its rage,

Against the winter of our age:
As he, the ancient Chief of Troy,
His manhood spent in peace and joy;
But Grecian fires, and loud alarms,
Called ancient Priam forth to arms.
Then happy those, since each must drain
His share of pleasure, share of pain,
Then happy those, beloved of Heaven,
To whom the mingled cup is given;
Whose lenient sorrows find relief,
Whose joys are chastened by their grief.
And such a lot, my Skene, was thine,
When thou, of late, wert doomed to twine—
Just when thy bridal hour was by—
The cypress with the myrtle tie.
Just on thy bride her sire had smiled,
And blessed the union of his child,
When Love must change its joyous cheer,
And wipe Affection's filial tear.
Nor did the actions next his end,
Speak more the father than the friend:
Scarce had lamented Forbes paid
The tribute to his minstrel's shade;
The tale of friendship scarce was told,
Ere the narrator's heart was cold—
Far may we search before we find
A heart so manly and so kind!
But not around his honoured urn
Shall friends alone and kindred mourn;
The thousand eyes his care had dried,
Pour at his name a bitter tide;
And frequent falls the grateful dew,
For benefits the world ne'er knew.
If mortal charity dare claim
The Almighty's attributed name,
Inscribe above his mouldering clay,
"The widow's shield, the orphan's stay."
Nor, though it wake thy sorrow, deem
My verse intrudes on this sad theme;

For sacred was the pen that wrote,
"Thy father's friend forget thou not:"
And grateful title may I plead,
For many a kindly word and deed,
To bring my tribute to his grave:—
'Tis little—but 'tis all I have.

  To thee, perchance, this rambling strain
Recalls our summer walks again;
When, doing naught—and, to speak true,
Not anxious to find aught to do—
The wild unbounded hills we ranged,
While oft our talk its topic changed,
And, desultory as our way,
Ranged, unconfined, from grave to gay.
Even when it flagged, as oft will chance,
No effort made to break its trance,
We could right pleasantly pursue
Our sports in social silence too;
Thou gravely labouring to portray
The blighted oak's fantastic spray;
I spelling o'er, with much delight,
The legend of that antique knight,
Tirante by name, ycleped the White.
At either's feet a trusty squire,
Pandour and Camp, with eyes of fire,
Jealous, each other's motions viewed,
And scarce suppressed their ancient feud.
The laverock whistled from the cloud;
The stream was lively, but not loud;
From the white thorn the Mayflower shed
Its dewy fragrance round our head:
Not Ariel lived more merrily
Under the blossomed bough than we.

  And blithesome nights, too, have been ours,
When winter stript the summer's bowers.
Careless we heard, what now I hear,
The wild blast sighing deep and drear,
When fires were bright, and lamps beamed gay,
And ladies tuned the lovely lay;

And he was held a laggard soul,
Who shunned to quaff the sparkling bowl.
Then he, whose absence we deplore,
Who breathes the gales of Devon's shore,
The longer missed, bewailed the more;
And thou, and I, and dear-loved Rae,
And one whose name I may not say—
For not Mimosa's tender tree
Shrinks sooner from the touch than he—
In merry chorus well combined,
With laughter drowned the whistling wind.
Mirth was within; and Care without
Might gnaw her nails to hear our shout.
Not but amid the buxom scene
Some grave discourse might intervene—
Of the good horse that bore him best,
His shoulder, hoof, and arching crest:
For, like mad Tom's, our chiefest care,
Was horse to ride, and weapon wear.
Such nights we've had; and, though the game
Of manhood be more sober tame,
And though the field-day, or the drill,
Seem less important now—yet still
Such may we hope to share again.
The sprightly thought inspires my strain!
And mark how, like a horseman true,
Lord Marmion's march I thus renew.

Canto Fourth

THE CAMP

I

EUSTACE, I said, did blithely mark
The first notes of the merry lark.
The lark sang shrill, the cock he crew,
And loudly Marmion's bugles blew,
And with their light and lively call,
Brought groom and yeoman to the stall.
　　Whistling they came, and free of heart,
　　　　But soon their mood was changed;
　　Complaint was heard on every part,
　　　　Of something disarranged.
Some clamoured loud for armour lost;
Some brawled and wrangled with the host;
"By Becket's bones," cried one, "I fear
That some false Scot has stol'n my spear!"
Young Blount, Lord Marmion's second squire,
Found his steed wet with sweat and mire;
Although the rated horse-boy sware,
Last night he dressed him sleek and fair.
While chafed the impatient squire like thunder,
Old Hubert shouts, in fear and wonder,
"Help, gentle Blount! help, comrades all!
Bevis lies dying in his stall:
To Marmion who the plight dare tell,
Of the good steed he loves so well?"
Gaping for fear and ruth, they saw
The charger panting on his straw;
Till one who would seem wisest, cried,
"What else but evil could betide,
With that cursed Palmer for our guide?
Better we had through mire and bush
Been lantern-led by Friar Rush."

II

Fitz-Eustace, who the cause but guessed,
    Nor wholly understood,
His comrades' clamorous plaints suppressed;
    He knew Lord Marmion's mood.
Him, ere he issued forth, he sought,
And found deep plunged in gloomy thought,
    And did his tale display
Simply, as if he knew of nought
    To cause such disarray.
Lord Marmion gave attention cold,
Nor marvelled at the wonders told—
Passed them as accidents of course,
And bade his clarions sound to horse.

III

Young Henry Blount, meanwhile, the cost
Had reckoned with their Scottish host;
And, as the charge he cast and paid,
"Ill thou deserv'st thy hire," he said;
"Dost see, thou knave, my horse's plight?
Fairies have ridden him all the night,
    And left him in a foam!
I trust that soon a conjuring band,
With English cross, and blazing brand,
Shall drive the devils from this land,
    To their infernal home:
For in this haunted den, I trow,
All night they trampled to and fro."
The laughing host looked on the hire—
"Gramercy, gentle southern squire,
And if thou com'st among the rest,
With Scottish broadsword to be blest,
Sharp be the brand, and sure the blow,
And short the pang to undergo."
Here stayed their talk; for Marmion
Gave now the signal to set on.

The Palmer showing forth the way,
They journeyed all the morning day.

IV

The greensward way was smooth and good,
Through Humbie's and through Saltoun's wood;
A forest glade, which, varying still,
Here gave a view of dale and hill,
There narrower closed, till overhead
A vaulted screen the branches made.
"A pleasant path," Fitz-Eustace said,
"Such as where errant-knights might see
Adventures of high chivalry;
Might meet some damsel flying fast,
With hair unbound, and looks aghast;
And smooth and level course were here,
In her defence to break a spear.
Here, too, are twilight nooks and dells;
And oft, in such, the story tells,
The damsel kind, from danger freed,
Did grateful pay her champion's meed."
He spoke to cheer Lord Marmion's mind;
Perchance to show his lore designed;
    For Eustace much had pored
Upon a huge romantic tome,
In the hall-window of his home,
Imprinted at the antique dome
    Of Caxton, or De Worde,
Therefore he spoke—but spoke in vain,
For Marmion answered nought again.

V

Now sudden, distant trumpets shrill,
In notes prolonged by wood and hill,
    Were heard to echo far:
Each ready archer grasped his bow,
But by the flourish soon they know,

They breathed no point of war.
Yet cautious, as in foeman's land,
Lord Marmion's order speeds the band,
    Some opener ground to gain;
And scarce a furlong had they rode,
When thinner trees, receding, showed
    A little woodland plain.
Just in that advantageous glade,
The halting troop a line had made,
As forth from the opposing shade
    Issued a gallant train.

VI

First came the trumpets, at whose clang
So late the forest echoes rang;
On prancing steeds they forward pressed,
With scarlet mantle, azure vest;
Each at his trump a banner wore,
Which Scotland's royal scutcheon bore:
Heralds and pursuivants, by name
Bute, Islay, Marchmount, Rothsay, came,
In painted tabards, proudly showing
Gules, argent, or, and azure glowing,
    Attendant on a king-at-arms,
Whose hand the armorial truncheon held,
That feudal strife had often quelled,
    When wildest its alarms.

VII

He was a man of middle age;
In aspect manly, grave, and sage,
    As on king's errand come;
But in the glances of his eye,
A penetrating, keen, and sly
    Expression found its home;
The flash of that satiric rage,
Which, bursting on the early stage,

Branded the vices of the age,
    And broke the keys of Rome.
On milk-white palfrey forth he paced;
His cap of maintenance was graced
    With the proud heron-plume.
From his steed's shoulder, loin, and breast,
    Silk housings swept the ground,
With Scotland's arms, device, and crest,
    Embroidered round and round.
The double tressure might you see,
    First by Achaius borne,
The thistle and the fleur-de-lis,
    And gallant unicorn.
So bright the king's armorial coat,
That scarce the dazzled eye could note,
In living colours, blazoned brave,
The lion, which his title gave;
A train, which well beseemed his state,
But all unarmed, around him wait.
    Still is thy name in high account,
        And still thy verse has charms,
    Sir David Lindesay of the Mount,
        Lord Lion King-at-Arms!

VIII

Down from his horse did Marmion spring,
Soon as he saw the Lion-King;
For well the stately baron knew
To him such courtesy was due,
Whom royal James himself had crowned,
And on his temples placed the round
    Of Scotland's ancient diadem;
And wet his brow with hallowed wine,
And on his finger given to shine
    The emblematic gem.
Their mutual greetings duly made,
The Lion thus his message said:—
"Though Scotland's king hath deeply swore

Ne'er to knit faith with Henry more,
And strictly hath forbid resort
From England to his royal court;
Yet, for he knows Lord Marmion's name,
And honours much his warlike fame,
My liege hath deemed it shame, and lack
Of courtesy, to turn him back:
And, by his order, I, your guide,
Must lodging fit and fair provide,
Till finds King James meet time to see
The flower of English chivalry."

IX

Though inly chafed at this delay,
Lord Marmion bears it as he may.
The Palmer, his mysterious guide,
Beholding thus his place supplied,
    Sought to take leave in vain:
Strict was the Lion-King's command,
That none, who rode in Marmion's band
    Should sever from the train:
"England has here enow of spies
In Lady Heron's witching eyes:"
To Marchmount thus, apart, he said,
But fair pretext to Marmion made.
The right hand path they now decline,
And trace against the stream the Tyne.

X

At length up that wild dale they wind,
    Where Crichtoun Castle crowns the bank;
For there the Lion's care assigned
    A lodging meet for Marmion's rank.
That castle rises on the steep
    Of the green vale of Tyne:
And far beneath, where slow they creep,
From pool to eddy, dark and deep,

Where alders moist, and willows weep,
     You hear her streams repine.
The towers in different ages rose;
Their various architecture shows
     The builders' various hands:
A mighty mass, that could oppose,
When deadliest hatred fired its foes,
     The vengeful Douglas bands.

XI

Crichtoun! though now thy miry court
     But pens the lazy steer and sheep,
     Thy turrets rude and tottered keep,
Have been the minstrel's loved resort.
Oft have I traced within thy fort,
     Of mouldering shields the mystic sense,
     Scutcheons of honour or pretence,
Quartered in old armorial sort,
     Remains of rude magnificence.
Nor wholly yet had time defaced
     Thy lordly gallery fair;
Nor yet the stony cord unbraced,
Whose twisted knots, with roses laced,
     Adorn thy ruined stair.
Still rises unimpaired below,
The courtyard's graceful portico;
Above its cornice, row and row
     Of fair hewn facets richly show
          Their pointed diamond form,
     Though there but houseless cattle go
          To shield them from the storm.
     And, shuddering, still may we explore,
          Where oft whilom were captives pent,
     The darkness of thy massy-more;
          Or, from thy grass-grown battlement,
May trace, in undulating line,
The sluggish mazes of the Tyne.

XII

Another aspect Crichtoun showed,
As through its portal Marmion rode;
But yet 'twas melancholy state
Received him at the outer gate;
For none were in the castle then,
But women, boys, or aged men.
With eyes scarce dried, the sorrowing dame,
To welcome noble Marmion came;
Her son, a stripling twelve years old,
Proffered the baron's rein to hold;
For each man that could draw a sword
Had marched that morning with their lord,
Earl Adam Hepburn—he who died
On Flodden, by his sovereign's side
Long may his lady look in vain!
She ne'er shall see his gallant train
Come sweeping back through Crichtoun Dean.
'Twas a brave race, before the name
Of hated Bothwell stained their fame.

XIII

And here two days did Marmion rest,
With every rite that honour claims,
Attended as the king's own guest;—
    Such the command of royal James,
Who marshalled then his land's array,
Upon the Borough Moor that lay.
Perchance he would not foeman's eye
Upon his gathering host should pry,
Till full prepared was every band
To march against the English land.
Here while they dwelt, did Lindesay's wit
Oft cheer the baron's moodier fit;
And, in his turn, he knew to prize
Lord Marmion's powerful mind, and wise—

Trained in the lore of Rome and Greece,
And policies of war and peace.

XIV

It chanced, as fell the second night,
    That on the battlements they walked,
And, by the slowly fading night,
    Of varying topics talked;
And, unaware, the herald-bard
Said, Marmion might his toil have spared,
    In travelling so far;
For that a messenger from heaven
In vain to James had counsel given
    Against the English war:
And, closer questioned, thus he told
A tale, which chronicles of old
In Scottish story have enrolled:—

XV

Sir David Lindesay's Tale

"Of all the palaces so fair,
    Built for the royal dwelling,
In Scotland far beyond compare,
    Linlithgow is excelling;
And in its park, in jovial June,
How sweet the merry linnet's tune,
    How blithe the blackbird's lay;
The wild-buck bells from ferny brake,
The coot dives merry on the lake;
The saddest heart might pleasure take
    To see all nature gay.
But June is, to our sovereign dear,
The heaviest month in all the year:
Too well his cause of grief you know,
June saw his father's overthrow,

Woe to the traitors, who could bring
The princely boy against his king!
Still in his conscience burns the sting.
In offices as strict as Lent,
King James's June is ever spent.

XVI

"When last this ruthful month was come,
And in Linlithgow's holy dome
    The King, as wont, was praying;
While, for his royal father's soul,
The chanters sung, the bells did toll,
    The bishop mass was saying—
For now the year brought round again
The day the luckless king was slain—
In Katharine's aisle the monarch knelt,
With sackcloth-shirt and iron belt,
    And eyes with sorrow streaming;
Around him, in their stalls of state,
The Thistle's knight-companions sate,
    Their banners o'er them beaming.
I too was there, and, sooth to tell,
Bedeafened with the jangling knell,
Was watching where the sunbeams fell,
    Through the stained casement gleaming;
But, while I marked what next befell,
    It seemed as I were dreaming.
Stepped from the crowd a ghostly wight,
In azure gown, with cincture white;
His forehead bald, his head was bare,
Down hung at length his yellow hair.
Now, mock me not, when, good my lord,
I pledged to you my knightly word,
That, when I saw his placid grace.
His simple majesty of face,
His solemn bearing, and his pace
    So stately gliding on,
Seemed to me ne'er did limner paint

So just an image of the Saint,
Who propped the Virgin in her faint—
    The loved Apostle John!

XVII

"He stepped before the monarch's chair,
And stood with rustic plainness there,
    And little reverence made:
Nor head, nor body, bowed nor bent,
But on the desk his arm he leant,
    And words like these he said,
In a low voice—but never tone
So thrilled through vein, and nerve, and bone:—
'My mother sent me from afar,
Sir King, to warn thee not to war—
    Woe waits on thine array;
If war thou wilt, of woman fair,
Her witching wiles and wanton snare,
James Stuart, doubly warned, beware:
    God keep thee as he may!'
The wondering monarch seemed to seek
    For answer, and found none;
And when he raised his head to speak,
    The monitor was gone.
The marshal and myself had cast
To stop him as he outward passed:
But, lighter than the whirlwind's blast,
    He vanished from our eyes,
Like sunbeam on the billow cast,
    That glances but, and dies."

XVIII

While Lindesay told his marvel strange,
    The twilight was so pale,
He marked not Marmion's colour change,
    While listening to the tale;
But, after a suspended pause,

The baron spoke:—"Of Nature's laws
　　So strong I held the force,
That never superhuman cause
　　Could e'er control their course;
And, three days since, had judged your aim
Was but to make your guest your game.
But I have seen, since passed the Tweed,
What much has changed my sceptic creed,
And made me credit aught." He stayed,
And seemed to wish his words unsaid:
But, by that strong emotion pressed,
Which prompts us to unload our breast,
　　E'en when discovery's pain,
To Lindesay did at length unfold
The tale his village host had told,
　　At Gifford, to his train.
Nought of the Palmer says he there,
And nought of Constance, or of Clare:
The thoughts which broke his sleep, he seems
To mention but as feverish dreams.

XIX

"In vain," said he, "to rest I spread
　My burning limbs, and couched my head:
　　Fantastic thoughts returned;
And, by their wild dominion led,
　　My heart within me burned.
So sore was the delirious goad,
I took my steed, and forth I rode,
And, as the moon shone bright and cold,
Soon reached the camp upon the wold.
The southern entrance I passed through,
And halted, and my bugle blew.
Methought an answer met my ear—
Yet was the blast so low and drear,
So hollow, and so faintly blown,
It might be echo of my own.

XX

"Thus judging, for a little space
I listened, ere I left the place;
    But scarce could trust my eyes,
Nor yet can think they served me true,
When sudden in the ring I view,
In form distinct of shape and hue,
    A mounted champion rise.
I've fought, Lord-Lion, many a day,
In single fight, and mixed affray,
And ever, I myself may say,
    Have borne me as a knight;
But when this unexpected foe
Seemed starting from the gulf below,
I care not though the truth I show,
    I trembled with affright;
And as I placed in rest my spear,
My hand so shook for very fear,
    I scarce could couch it right.

XXI

"Why need my tongue the issue tell?
We ran our course—my charger fell;
What could he 'gainst the shock of hell?
    I rolled upon the plain.
High o'er my head, with threatening hand,
The spectre took his naked brand—
    Yet did the worst remain:
My dazzled eyes I upward cast—
Not opening hell itself could blast
    Their sight, like what I saw!
Full on his face the moonbeam strook—
A face could never be mistook!
I knew the stern vindictive look,
    And held my breath for awe.
I saw the face of one who, fled
To foreign climes, has long been dead—

I well believe the last;
For ne'er, from vizor raised, did stare
A human warrior, with a glare
    So grimly and so ghast.
Thrice o'er my head he shook the blade;
.But when to good Saint George I prayed,
The first time e'er I asked his aid,
    He plunged it in the sheath;
And, on his courser mounting light,
He seemed to vanish from my sight;
The moonbeam drooped, and deepest night
    Sunk down upon the heath.
'Twere long to tell what cause I have
    To know his face, that met me there,
Called by his hatred from the grave,
    To cumber upper air;
Dead or alive, good cause had he
To be my mortal enemy."

XXII

Marvelled Sir David of the Mount;
Then, learned in story, 'gan recount
    Such chance had happed of old,
When once, near Norham, there did fight
A spectre fell of fiendish might,
In likeness of a Scottish knight,
    With Brian Bulmer bold,
And trained him nigh to disallow
The aid of his baptismal vow.
"And such a phantom, too, 'tis said,
With Highland broadsword, targe, and plaid,
    And fingers red with gore,
Is seen in Rothiemurcus glade,
Or where the sable pine-trees' shade
Dark Tomantoul, and Auchnaslaid,
    Dromunchty, or Glenmore.
And yet whate'er such legends say,
Of warlike demon, ghost, or fay,

On mountain, moor, or plain,
Spotless in faith, in bosom bold,
True son of chivalry should hold
    These midnight terrors vain;
For seldom hath such spirit power
To harm, save in the evil hour,
When guilt we meditate within,
Or harbour unrepented sin."
Lord Marmion turned him half aside,
And twice to clear his voice he tried,
    Then pressed Sir David's hand—
But nought at length in answer said,
And here their farther converse stayed,
    Each ordering that his band
Should bowne them with the rising day,
To Scotland's camp to take their way—
    Such was the King's command.

XXIII

Early they took Dunedin's road,
And I could trace each step they trode;
Hill, brook, nor dell, nor rock, nor stone,
Lies on the path to me unknown.
Much might it boast of storied lore;
But, passing such digression o'er,
Suffice it that their route was laid
Across the furzy hills of Braid,
They passed the glen and scanty rill,
And climbed the opposing bank, until
They gained the top of Blackford Hill.

XXIV

Blackford! on whose uncultured breast,
    Among the broom, and thorn, and whin,
A truant-boy, I sought the nest,
Or listed, as I lay at rest,
    While rose on breezes thin,

The murmur of the city crowd,
And, from his steeple jangling loud,
    Saint Giles's mingling din.
Now, from the summit to the plain,
Waves all the hill with yellow grain
    And o'er the landscape as I look,
Nought do I see unchanged remain,
    Save the rude cliffs and chiming brook.
To me they make a heavy moan,
Of early friendships past and gone.

XXV

But different far the change has been,
    Since Marmion, from the crown
Of Blackford, saw that martial scene
    Upon the bent so brown:
Thousand pavilions, white as snow,
Spread all the Borough Moor below,
    Upland, and dale, and down:—
A thousand, did I say? I ween,
Thousands on thousands there were seen,
That chequered all the heath between
    The streamlet and the town;
In crossing ranks extending far,
Forming a camp irregular;
Oft giving way, where still there stood
Some relics of the old oak wood,
That darkly huge did intervene,
And tamed the glaring white with green:
In these extended lines there lay
A martial kingdom's vast array.

XXVI

For from Hebudes, dark with rain,
To eastern Lodon's fertile plain,
And from the southern Redswire edge,
To farthest Rosse's rocky ledge;

From west to east, from south to north.
Scotland sent all her warriors forth.
Marmion might hear the mingled hum
Of myriads up the mountain come;
The horses' tramp, and tingling clank,
Where chiefs reviewed their vassal rank,
 And charger's shrilling neigh;
And see the shifting lines advance
While frequent flashed, from shield and lance,
 The sun's reflected ray.

XXVII

Thin curling in the morning air,
The wreaths of failing smoke declare,
To embers now the brands decayed,
Where the night-watch their fires had made.
They saw, slow rolling on the plain,
Full many a baggage-cart and wain,
And dire artillery's clumsy car,
By sluggish oxen tugged to war;
And there were Borthwick's Sisters Seven,
And culverins which France had given.
Ill-omened gift! the guns remain
The conqueror's spoil on Flodden plain.

XXVIII

Nor marked they less, where in the air
A thousand streamers flaunted fair;
 Various in shape, device, and hue,
 Green, sanguine, purple, red, and blue,
Broad, narrow, swallow-tailed, and square,
Scroll, pennon, pensil, bandrol, there
 O'er the pavilions flew.
Highest and midmost, was descried
The royal banner floating wide;
 The staff, a pine-tree strong and straight,
Pitched deeply in a massive stone—

Which still in memory is shown—
 Yet bent beneath the standard's weight
  Whene'er the western wind unrolled,
 With toil, the huge and cumbrous fold,
And gave to view the dazzling field,
Where, in proud Scotland's royal shield,
 The ruddy lion ramped in gold.

XXIX

Lord Marmion viewed the landscape bright—
He viewed it with a chief's delight—
 Until within him burned his heart
 And lightning from his eye did part,
  As on the battle-day;
 Such glance did falcon never dart,
  When stooping on his prey.
"Oh! well, Lord Lion, hast thou said,
Thy king from warfare to dissuade
 Were but a vain essay:
For, by Saint George, were that host mine,
Not power infernal, nor divine.
Should once to peace my soul incline,
Till I had dimmed their armour's shine
 In glorious battle-fray!"
Answered the bard, of milder mood—
"Fair is the sight—and yet 'twere good
 That kings would think withal,
When peace and wealth their land has blessed,
'Tis better to sit still at rest,
Than rise, perchance to fall."

XXX

Still on the spot Lord Marmion stayed,
For fairer scene he ne'er surveyed.
 When sated with the martial show
 That peopled all the plain below,
 The wandering eye could o'er it go,

And mark the distant city glow
    With gloomy splendour red;
For on the smoke-wreaths, huge and slow,
That round her sable turrets flow,
    The morning beams were shed,
And tinged them with a lustre proud,
Like that which streaks a thunder-cloud.
Such dusky grandeur clothed the height,
Where the huge castle holds its state,
    And all the steep slope down,
Whose ridgy back heaves to the sky,
Piled deep and massy, close and high,
    Mine own romantic town!
But northward far, with purer blaze,
On Ochil mountains fell the rays,
And as each heathy top they kissed,
It gleamed a purple amethyst.
Yonder the shores of Fife you saw;
Here Preston Bay and Berwick Law:
    And, broad between them rolled,
The gallant Frith the eye might note,
Whose islands on its bosom float,
    Like emeralds chased in gold.
Fitz Eustace' heart felt closely pent;
As if to give his rapture vent,
The spur he to his charger lent,
    And raised his bridle hand,
And making demivolte in air,
Cried, "Where's the coward that would not dare
    To fight for such a land!"
The Lindesay smiled his joy to see;
Nor Marmion's frown repressed his glee.

XXXI

Thus while they looked, a flourish proud,
Where mingled trump and clarion loud,
    And fife and kettle-drum,
And sackbut deep, and psaltery,

And war-pipe with discordant cry,
And cymbal clattering to the sky,
Making wild music bold and high,
    Did up the mountain come;
The whilst the bells, with distant chime,
Merrily tolled the hour of prime,
    And thus the Lindesay spoke:
"Thus clamour still the war-notes when
The King to mass his way has ta'en,
Or to St. Katharine's of Sienne,
    Or chapel of Saint Rocque.
To you they speak of martial fame;
But me remind of peaceful game,
    When blither was their cheer,
Thrilling in Falkland woods the air,
In signal none his steed should spare,
But strive which foremost might repair
    To the downfall of the deer.

XXXII

"Nor less," he said, "when looking forth,
I view yon empress of the North
    Sit on her hilly throne;
Her palace's imperial bowers,
Her castle, proof to hostile powers,
Her stately halls and holy towers—
    Nor less," he said, "I moan,
To think what woe mischance may bring,
And how these merry bells may ring
The death-dirge of our gallant king;
    Or with the 'larum call
The burghers forth to watch and ward,
'Gainst Southern sack and fires to guard
    Dunedin's leaguered wall.
But not for my presaging thought,
Dream conquest sure, or cheaply bought!
    Lord Marmion, I say nay:
God is the guider of the field,

He breaks the champion's spear and shield—
    But thou thyself shalt say,
When joins yon host in deadly stowre,
That England's dames must weep in bower,
    Her monks the death-mass sing;
For never saw'st thou such a power
    Led on by such a king."
And now, down winding to the plain,
The barriers of the camp they gain,
    And there they made a stay.
There stays the minstrel, till he fling
His hand o'er every Border string,
And fit his harp the pomp to sing,
Of Scotland's ancient court and king,
    In the succeeding lay.

Introduction to Canto Fifth

To George Ellis, Esq.

—Edinburgh

When dark December glooms the day,
And takes our autumn joys away;
When short and scant the sunbeam throws,
Upon the weary waste of snows,
A cold and profitless regard,
Like patron on a needy bard,
When silvan occupation's done,
And o'er the chimney rests the gun,
And hang, in idle trophy, near,
The game-pouch, fishing-rod, and spear;
When wiry terrier, rough and grim,
And greyhound, with his length of limb,
And pointer, now employed no more,
Cumber our parlour's narrow floor;
When in his stall the impatient steed
Is long condemned to rest and feed;
When from our snow-encircled home,
Scarce cares the hardiest step to roam,
Since path is none, save that to bring
The needful water from the spring;
When wrinkled news-page, thrice conned o'er,
Beguiles the dreary hour no more,
And darkling politican, crossed
Inveighs against the lingering post,
And answering housewife sore complains
Of carriers' snow-impeded wains;
When such the country cheer, I come,
Well pleased, to seek our city home;
For converse, and for books, to change
The Forest's melancholy range,
And welcome, with renewed delight,
The busy day and social night.

Not here need my desponding rhyme
Lament the ravages of time,
As erst by Newark's riven towers,
And Ettrick stripped of forest bowers.
True—Caledonia's Queen is changed,
Since on her dusky summit ranged,
Within its steepy limits pent,
By bulwark, line, and battlement,
And flanking towers, and laky flood,
Guarded and garrisoned she stood,
Denying entrance or resort,
Save at each tall embattled port;
Above whose arch, suspended, hung
Portcullis spiked with iron prong.
That long is gone,—but not so long,
Since, early closed, and opening late,
Jealous revolved the studded gate,
Whose task, from eve to morning tide,
A wicket churlishly supplied.
Stern then, and steel-girt was thy brow,
Dunedin! Oh, how altered now,
When safe amid thy mountain court
Thou sitt'st, like empress at her sport,
And liberal, unconfined, and free,
Flinging thy white arms to the sea,
For thy dark cloud, with umbered lower,
That hung o'er cliff, and lake, and tower,
Thou gleam'st against the western ray
Ten thousand lines of brighter day.

Not she, the championess of old,
In Spenser's magic tale enrolled,
She for the charméd spear renowned,
Which forced each knight to kiss the ground—
Not she more changed, when, placed at rest,
What time she was Malbecco's guest,
She gave to flow her maiden vest;
When from the corslet's grasp relieved,
Free to the sight her bosom heaved;
Sweet was her blue eye's modest smile,

Erst hidden by the aventayle;
And down her shoulders graceful rolled
Her locks profuse, of paly gold.
They who whilom, in midnight fight,
Had marvelled at her matchless might,
No less her maiden charms approved,
But looking liked, and liking loved.
The sight could jealous pangs beguile,
And charm Malbecco's cares a while;
And he, the wandering squire of dames,
Forgot his Columbella's claims,
And passion, erst unknown, could gain
The breast of blunt Sir Satyrane;
Nor durst light Paridel advance,
Bold as he was, a looser glance.
She charmed at once, and tamed the heart,
Incomparable Britomarte!

    So thou, fair city! disarrayed
Of battled wall, and rampart's aid,
As stately seem'st, but lovelier far
Than in that panoply of war.
Nor deem that from thy fenceless throne
Strength and security are flown;
Still as of yore Queen of the North!
Still canst thou send thy children forth.
Ne'er readier at alarm-bell's call
Thy burghers rose to man thy wall,
Than now, in danger, shall be thine,
Thy dauntless voluntary line;
For fosse and turret proud to stand,
Their breasts the bulwarks of the land.
Thy thousands, trained to martial toil,
Full red would stain their native soil,
Ere from thy mural crown there fell
The slightest knosp or pinnacle.
And if it come—as come it may,
Dunedin! that eventful day—
Renowned for hospitable deed,
That virtue much with Heaven may plead

In patriarchal times whose care
Descending angels deigned to share;
That claim may wrestle blessings down
On those who fight for the good town,
Destined in every age to be
Refuge of injured royalty;
Since first, when conquering York arose,
To Henry meek she gave repose,
Till late, with wonder, grief, and awe,
Great Bourbon's relics, sad she saw.

    Truce to these thoughts!—for, as they rise,
How gladly I avert mine eyes,
Bodings, or true or false, to change,
For Fiction's fair romantic range,
Or for tradition's dubious light,
That hovers 'twixt the day and night:
Dazzling alternately and dim,
Her wavering lamp I'd rather trim,
Knights, squires, and lovely dames, to see
Creation of my fantasy,
Than gaze abroad on reeky fen,
And make of mists invading men.
Who love not more the night of June
Than dull December's gloomy noon?
The moonlight than the fog of frost?
And can we say which cheats the most?

    But who shall teach my harp to gain
A sound of the romantic strain,
Whose Anglo-Norman tones whilere
Could win the royal Henry's ear,
Famed Beauclerc called, for that he loved
The minstrel, and his lay approved?
Who shall these lingering notes redeem,
Decaying on Oblivion's stream;
Such notes as from the Breton tongue
Marie translated, Blondel sung?
O! born Time's ravage to repair,
And make the dying muse thy care;
Who, when his scythe her hoary foe

Was poising for the final blow,
The weapon from his hand could wring,
And break his glass, and shear his wing,
And bid, reviving in his strain,
The gentle poet live again;
Thou, who canst give to lightest lay
An unpedantic moral gay,
Nor less the dullest theme bid flit
On wings of unexpected wit;
In letters as in life approved,
Example honoured and beloved—
Dear Ellis! to the bard impart
A lesson of thy magic art,
To win at once the head and heart—
At once to charm, instruct, and mend,
My guide, my pattern, and my friend!

    Such minstrel lesson to bestow
Be long thy pleasing task—but, oh!
No more by thy example teach—
What few can practise, all can preach—
With even patience to endure
Lingering disease, and painful cure,
And boast affliction's pangs subdued
By mild and manly fortitude.
Enough, the lesson has been given:
Forbid the repetition, Heaven!

    Come, listen, then! for thou hast known,
And loved the minstrel's varying tone,
Who, like his Border sires of old,
Waked a wild measure rude and bold,
Till Windsor's oaks, and Ascot plain,
With wonder heard the Northern strain.
Come, listen! bold in thy applause,
The bard shall scorn pedantic laws;
And, as the ancient art could stain
Achievements on the storied pane,
Irregularly traced and planned,
But yet so glowing and so grand—

So shall he strive in changeful hue,
Field, feast, and combat to renew,
And loves, and arms, and harpers' glee,
And all the pomp of chivalry.

Canto Fifth

THE COURT

I

THE train has left the hills of Braid;
The barrier guard have open made
   (So Lindesay bade) the palisade,
That closed the tented ground;
Their men the warders backward drew,
And carried pikes as they rode through
   Into its ample bound.
Fast ran the Scottish warriors there,
Upon the Southern band to stare.
And envy with their wonder rose,
To see such well-appointed foes;
Such length of shaft, such mighty bows,
So huge, that many simply thought,
But for a vaunt such weapons wrought;
And little deemed their force to feel,
Through links of mail, and plates of steel,
When rattling upon Flodden vale,
The clothyard arrows flew like hail.

II

Nor less did Marmion's skilful view
Glance every line and squadron through;
And much he marvelled one small land
Could marshal forth such various band:
   For men-at-arms were here,
Heavily sheathed in mail and plate,
Like iron towers for strength and weight,
On Flemish steeds of bone and height,
   With battle-axe and spear.
Young knights and squires, a lighter train,

Practised their chargers on the plain,
By aid of leg, of hand, and rein,
    Each warlike feat to show,
To pass, to wheel, the croupe to gain,
The high curvet, that not in vain
The sword sway might descend amain
    On foeman's casque below.
He saw the hardy burghers there
March armed, on foot, with faces bare,
    For vizor they wore none,
Nor waving plume, nor crest of knight;
But burnished were their corslets bright,
Their brigantines, and gorgets light,
    Like very silver shone.
Long pikes they had for standing fight,
    Two-handed swords they wore,
And many wielded mace of weight,
    And bucklers bright they bore.

III

On foot the yeomen too, but dressed
In his steel-jack, a swarthy vest,
    With iron quilted well;
Each at his back (a slender store)
His forty days' provision bore,
    As feudal statutes tell.
His arms were halbert, axe, or spear,
A crossbow there, a hagbut here,
    A dagger-knife, and brand.
Sober he seemed, and sad of cheer,
As loth to leave his cottage dear,
    And march to foreign strand;
Or musing who would guide his steer
    To till the fallow land.
Yet deem not in his thoughtful eye
Did aught of dastard terror lie;
    More dreadful far his ire
Than theirs, who, scorning danger's name,

In eager mood to battle came,
Their valour like light straw on flame,
    A fierce but fading fire.

IV

Not so the Borderer:—bred to war,
He knew the battle's din afar,
    And joyed to hear it swell.
His peaceful day was slothful ease;
Nor harp, nor pipe, his ear could please
    Like the loud slogan yell.
On active steed, with lance and blade,
The light-armed pricker plied his trade—
    Let nobles fight for fame;
Let vassals follow where they lead,
Burghers to guard their townships bleed,
    But war's the Borderer's game.
Their gain, their glory, their delight,
To sleep the day, maraud the night
    O'er mountain, moss, and moor;
Joyful to fight they took their way,
Scarce caring who might win the day,
    Their booty was secure.
These, as Lord Marmion's train passed by,
Looked on at first with careless eye,
Nor marvelled aught, well taught to know
The form and force of English bow;
But when they saw the lord arrayed
In splendid arms and rich brocade,
Each Borderer to his kinsman said:—
    "Hist, Ringan! seest thou there!
Canst guess which road they'll homeward ride?
Oh! could we but on Border side,
By Eusedale glen, or Liddell's tide,
    Beset a prize so fair!
That fangless Lion, too, their guide,
Might chance to lose his glistering hide;

Brown Maudlin, of that doublet pied
    Could make a kirtle rare."

V

Next, Marmion marked the Celtic race,
Of different language, form, and face—
    Avarious race of man;
Just then the chiefs their tribes arrayed,
And wild and garish semblance made
The chequered trews and belted plaid,
And varying notes the war-pipes brayed
    To every varying clan;
Wild through their red or sable hair
Looked out their eyes with savage stare
    On Marmion as he passed;
Their legs above the knee were bare;
Their frame was sinewy, short, and spare,
    And hardened to the blast;
Of taller race, the chiefs they own
Were by the eagle's plumage known.
The hunted red-deer's undressed hide
Their hairy buskins well supplied;
The graceful bonnet decked their head;
Back from their shoulders hung the plaid;
A broadsword of unwieldy length,
A dagger proved for edge and strength,
    A studded targe they wore,
And quivers, bows, and shafts,—but, oh!
Short was the shaft and weak the bow
    To that which England bore.
The Islesmen carried at their backs
The ancient Danish battle-axe.
They raised a wild and wondering cry
As with his guide rode Marmion by.
Loud were their clamouring tongues, as when
The clanging sea-fowl leave the fen,
And, with their cries discordant mixed,
Grumbled and yelled the pipes betwixt.

Thus through the Scottish camp they passed,
And reached the city gate at last,
Where all around, a wakeful guard,
Armed burghers kept their watch and ward.
Well had they cause of jealous fear,
When lay encamped, in field so near,
The Borderer and the Mountaineer.
As through the bustling streets they go,
All was alive with martial show;
At every turn, with dinning clang,
The armourer's anvil clashed and rang;
Or toiled the swarthy smith, to wheel
The bar that arms the charger's heel;
Or axe or falchion to the side
Of jarring grindstone was applied.
Page, groom, and squire, with hurrying pace,
Through street and lane and market-place
    Bore lance, or casque, or sword;
While burghers, with important face,
    Described each new-come lord,
Discussed his lineage, told his name,
His following and his warlike fame.
The Lion led to lodging meet,
Which high o'erlooked the crowded street;
    There must the baron rest
Till past the hour of vesper tide,
And then to Holyrood must ride—
    Such was the king's behest.
Meanwhile the Lion's care assigns
A banquet rich, and costly wines,
    To Marmion and his train;
And when the appointed hour succeeds,
The baron dons his peaceful weeds,
And following Lindesay as he leads,
    The palace-halls they gain.

VII

Old Holyrood rung merrily
That night with wassail, mirth, and glee:
King James within her princely bower
Feasted the chiefs of Scotland's power,
Summoned to spend the parting hour;
For he had charged that his array
Should southward march by break of day.
Well loved that splendid monarch aye
 The banquet and the song,
By day the tourney, and by night
The merry dance, traced fast and light,
The maskers quaint, the pageant bright,
 The revel loud and long.
This feast outshone his banquets past:
It was his blithest—and his last.
The dazzling lamps, from gallery gay,
Cast on the Court a dancing ray;
Here to the harp did minstrels sing;
There ladies touched a softer string;
With long-eared cap and motley vest
The licensed fool retailed his jest;
His magic tricks the juggler plied;
At dice and draughts the gallants vied;
While some, in close recess apart,
Courted the ladies of their heart,
 Nor courted them in vain;
For often in the parting hour
Victorious Love asserts his power
 O'er coldness and disdain;
And flinty is her heart, can view
To battle march a lover true—
Can hear, perchance, his last adieu,
 Nor own her share of pain.

VIII

Through this mixed crowd of glee and game,
The King to greet Lord Marmion came,
    While, reverent, all made room.
An easy task it was, I trow,
King James's manly form to know,
Although, his courtesy to show,
He doffed, to Marmion bending low,
    His broidered cap and plume.
For royal was his garb and mien:
    His cloak, of crimson velvet piled.
    Trimmed with the fur of martin wild;
His vest of changeful satin sheen
    The dazzled eye beguiled;
His gorgeous collar hung adown,
Wrought with the badge of Scotland's crown,
The thistle brave, of old renown;
His trusty blade, Toledo right,
Descended from a baldric bright:
White were his buskins, on the heel
His spurs inlaid of gold and steel;
His bonnet, all of crimson fair,
Was buttoned with a ruby rare:
And Marmion deemed he ne'er had seen
A prince of such a noble mien.

IX

The monarch's form was middle size:
For feat of strength or exercise
    Shaped in proportion fair;
And hazel was his eagle eye,
And auburn of the darkest dye
    His short curled beard and hair.
Light was his footstep in the dance,
    And firm his stirrup in the lists:
And, oh! he had that merry glance
    That seldom lady's heart resists.

Lightly from fair to fair he flew,
And loved to plead, lament, and sue—
Suit lightly won and short-lived pain,
For monarchs seldom sigh in vain.
    I said he joyed in banquet bower;
But, 'mid his mirth, 'twas often strange
How suddenly his cheer would change,
    His look o'ercast and lower,
If, in a sudden turn, he felt
The pressure of his iron belt,
That bound his breast in penance pain,
In memory of his father slain.
Even so 'twas strange how, evermore,
Soon as the passing pang was o'er
Forward he rushed, with double glee,
Into the stream of revelry:
Thus dim-seen object of affright
Startles the courser in his flight,
And half he halts, half springs aside;
But feels the quickening spur applied,
And, straining on the tightened rein,
Scours doubly swift o'er hill and plain.

                    X

O'er James's heart, the courtiers say,
Sir Hugh the Heron's wife held sway:
    To Scotland's Court she came,
To be a hostage for her lord,
Who Cessford's gallant heart had gored,
And with the king to make accord
    Had sent his lovely dame.
Nor to that lady free alone
Did the gay king allegiance own;
    For the fair Queen of France
Sent him a turquoise ring and glove,
And charged him, as her knight and love,
    For her to break a lance;
And strike three strokes with Scottish brand,

And march three miles on Southron land,
And bid the banners of his band
   In English breezes dance.
And thus for France's queen he drest
His manly limbs in mailèd vest;
And thus admitted English fair
His inmost counsels still to share:
And thus, for both, he madly planned
The ruin of himself and land!
   And yet, the sooth to tell,
Nor England's fair, nor France's Queen,
Were worth one pearl-drop, bright and sheen,
   From Margaret's eyes that fell,
His own Queen Margaret, who, in Lithgow's bower,
All lonely sat, and wept the weary hour.

XI

The queen sits lone in Lithgow pile,
And weeps the weary day,
The war against her native soil,
Her monarch's risk in battle broil;
And in gay Holyrood the while
Dame Heron rises with a smile
   Upon the harp to play.
Fair was her rounded arm, as o'er
   The strings her fingers flew;
And as she touched and tuned them all,
Ever her bosom's rise and fall
   Was plainer given to view;
For, all for heat, was laid aside
Her wimple, and her hood untied.
And first she pitched her voice to sing,
Then glanced her dark eye on the king,
And then around the silent ring;
And laughed, and blushed, and oft did say
Her pretty oath, By yea and nay,
She could not, would not, durst not play!
At length upon the harp with glee,

Mingled with arch simplicity,
A soft yet lively air she rung,
While thus the wily lady sung:—

XII

LOCHINVAR

Oh! young Lochinvar is come out of the west,
Through all the wide Border his steed was the best;
And save his good broadsword, he weapons had none,
He rode all unarmed, and he rode all alone;
So faithful in love, and so dauntless in war,
There never was knight like the young Lochinvar.

He stayed not for brake, and he stopped not for stone;
He swam the Esk river, where ford there was none;
But ere he alighted at Netherby gate,
The bride had consented, the gallant came late;
For a laggard in love, and a dastard in war,
Was to wed the fair Ellen of brave Lochinvar.

So boldly he entered the Netherby Hall,
Among bride's-men, and kinsmen, and brothers, and all;
Then spoke the bride's father, his hand on his sword—
For the poor craven bridegroom said never a word—
"Oh! come ye in peace here, or come ye in war,
Or to dance at our bridal, young Lord Lochinvar?"

"I long wooed your daughter, my suit you denied;
Love swells like the Solway, but ebbs like its tide;
And now am I come, with this lost love of mine,
To lead but one measure, drink one cup of wine.
There are maidens in Scotland more lovely by far,
That would gladly be bride to the young Lochinvar."

The bride kissed the goblet: the knight took it up,
He quaffed off the wine, and he threw down the cup.
She looked down to blush, and she looked up to sigh,

With a smile on her lips and a tear in her eye.
He took her soft hand, ere her mother could bar—
"Now tread we a measure!" said young Lochinvar.

So stately his form, and so lovely her face,
That never a hall such a galliard did grace;
While her mother did fret, and her father did fume,
And the bridegroom stood dangling his bonnet and plume:
And the bride's-maidens whispered, "'Twere better by far
To have matched our fair cousin with young Lochinvar."

One touch to her hand, and one word in her ear,
When they reached the hall-door, and the charger stood near;
So light to the croup the fair lady he swung,
So light to the saddle before her he sprung.
"She is won! we are gone, over bank, bush, and scaur;
They'll have fleet steeds that follow," quoth young Lochinvar.

There was mounting 'mong Graemes of the Netherby clan;
Forsters, Fenwicks, and Musgraves, they rode and they ran:
There was racing and chasing on Cannobie Lee,
But the lost bride of Netherby ne'er did they see.
So daring in love, and so dauntless in war,
Have ye e'er heard of gallant like young Lochinvar?

XIII

The monarch o'er the siren hung,
And beat the measure as she sung;
And, pressing closer and more near,
He whispered praises in her ear.
In loud applause the courtiers vied,
And ladies winked and spoke aside.
 The witching dame to Marmion threw
  A glance, where seemed to reign
 The pride that claims applauses due,
 And of her royal conquest too,
  A real or feigned disdain:
Familiar was the look, and told

Marmion and she were friends of old.
The king observed their meeting eyes
With something like displeased surprise:
For monarchs ill can rivals brook,
E'en in a word or smile or look.
Straight took he forth the parchment broad
Which Marmion's high commission showed:
"Our Borders sacked by many a raid,
 Our peaceful liegemen robbed," he said;
"On day of truce our warden slain,
 Stout Barton killed, his vassals ta'en—
 Unworthy were we here to reign,
 Should these for vengeance cry in vain;
 Our full defiance, hate, and scorn,
 Our herald has to Henry borne."

XIV

He paused, and led where Douglas stood,
And with stern eye the pageant viewed—
I mean that Douglas, sixth of yore,
Who coronet of Angus bore,
And, when his blood and heart were high,
Did the third James in camp defy,
And all his minions led to die
      On Lauder's dreary flat:
Princes and favourites long grew tame,
And trembled at the homely name
      Of Archibald Bell-the-Cat;
The same who left the dusky vale
Of Hermitage in Liddisdale,
      Its dungeons and its towers,
Where Bothwell's turrets brave the air,
And Bothwell bank is blooming fair,
      To fix his princely bowers.
Though now in age he had laid down
His armour for the peaceful gown,
      And for a staff his brand,
Yet often would flash forth the fire

That could in youth a monarch's ire
    And minion's pride withstand;
And e'en that day, at council board,
    Unapt to soothe his sovereign's mood,
    Against the war had Angus stood,
And chafed his royal lord.

XV

    His giant form like ruined tower,
Though fall'n its muscles' brawny vaunt,
Huge-boned, and tall, and grim, and gaunt,
    Seemed o'er the gaudy scene to lower:
His locks and beard in silver grew;
His eyebrows kept their sable hue.
Near Douglas when the monarch stood,
His bitter speech he thus pursued:
"Lord Marmion, since these letters say
That in the north you needs must stay
    While slightest hopes of peace remain,
Uncourteous speech it were, and stern,
To say—return to Lindisfarne
    Until my herald come again.
Then rest you in Tantallon Hold;
Your host shall be the Douglas bold—
A chief unlike his sires of old.
He wears their motto on his blade,
Their blazon o'er his towers displayed;
Yet loves his sovereign to oppose,
More than to face his country's foes.
    And, I bethink me, by Saint Stephen,
But e'en this morn to me was given
A prize, the first-fruits of the war,
Ta'en by a galley from Dunbar,
    A bevy of the maids of Heaven.
Under your guard these holy maids
Shall safe return to cloister shades;
And, while they at Tantallon stay,
Requiem for Cochrane's soul may say."

And with the slaughtered favourite's name
Across the monarch's brow there came
A cloud of ire, remorse, and shame.

XVI

In answer nought could Angus speak;
His proud heart swelled well-nigh to break:
He turned aside, and down his cheek
 A burning tear there stole.
His hand the monarch sudden took;
That sight his kind heart could not brook:
 "Now, by the Bruce's soul,
Angus, my hasty speech forgive!
For sure as doth his spirit live,
As he said of the Douglas old,
 I well may say of you—
That never king did subject hold
In speech more free, in war more bold,
 More tender and more true:
Forgive me, Douglas, once again."
And while the king his hand did strain,
The old man's tears fell down like rain.
To seize the moment Marmion tried,
And whispered to the king aside:
"Oh! let such tears unwonted plead
For respite short from dubious deed!
A child will weep a bramble's smart,
A maid to see her sparrow part,
A stripling for a woman's heart:
But woe awaits a country when
She sees the tears of bearded men.
Then, oh! what omen, dark and high,
When Douglas wets his manly eye!"

XVII

Displeased was James, that stranger viewed
And tampered with his changing mood.

"Laugh those that can, weep those that may,"
Thus did the fiery monarch say,
"Southward I march by break of day;
And if within Tantallon strong,
The good Lord Marmion tarries long,
Perchance our meeting next may fall
At Tamworth, in his castle-hall."
The haughty Marmion felt the taunt,
And answered, grave, the royal vaunt:—
"Much honoured were my humble home
If in its halls King James should come;
But Nottingham has archers good,
And Yorkshire-men are stern of mood;
Northumbrian prickers wild and rude.
On Derby hills the paths are steep;
In Ouse and Tyne the fords are deep;
And many a banner will be torn,
And many a knight to earth be borne,
And many a sheaf of arrows spent,
Ere Scotland's king shall cross the Trent:
Yet pause, brave prince, while yet you may."
The monarch lightly turned away,
And to his nobles loud did call,
"Lords, to the dance—a hall! a hall!"
Himself his cloak and sword flung by,
And led Dame Heron gallantly;
And minstrels, at the royal order,
Rung out "Blue Bonnets o'er the Border."

XVIII

Leave we these revels now, to tell
What to Saint Hilda's maids befell,
Whose galley, as they sailed again
To Whitby, by a Scot was ta'en.
Now at Dunedin did they bide,
Till James should of their fate decide;
    And soon, by his command,
Were gently summoned to prepare

To journey under Marmion's care,
As escort honoured, safe, and fair,
     Again to English land.
The Abbess told her chaplet o'er,
Nor knew which saint she should implore;
For when she thought of Constance, sore
     She feared Lord Marmion's mood.
And judge what Clara must have felt!
The sword that hung in Marmion's belt
     Had drunk De Wilton's blood.
Unwittingly, King James had given,
     As guard to Whitby's shades,
The man most dreaded under heaven
     By these defenceless maids:
Yet what petition could avail,
Or who would listen to the tale
Of woman, prisoner, and nun,
'Mid bustle of a war begun?
They deemed it hopeless to avoid
The convoy of their dangerous guide.

XIX

Their lodging, so the king assigned,
To Marmion's, as their guardian, joined;
And thus it fell that, passing nigh,
The Palmer caught the Abbess' eye,
     Who warned him by a scroll
She had a secret to reveal
That much concerned the Church's weal
     And health of sinner's soul;
And with deep charge of secrecy
     She named a place to meet,
Within an open balcony
That hung from dizzy pitch, and high
     Above the stately street;
To which, as common to each home,
At night they might in secret come.

XX

At night, in secret, there they came,
The Palmer and the holy dame.
The moon among the clouds rose high,
And all the city hum was by.
Upon the street, where late before
Did din of war and warriors roar,
    You might have heard a pebble fall,
A beetle hum, a cricket sing,
An owlet flap his boding wing
    On Giles's steeple tall.
The antique buildings, climbing high,
Whose Gothic frontlets sought the sky,
    Were here wrapt deep in shade;
There on their brows the moonbeam broke
Through the faint wreaths of silvery smoke,
    And on the casements played.
    And other light was none to see,
      Save torches gliding far,
    Before some chieftain of degree,
    Who left the royal revelry
      To bowne him for the war.
A solemn scene the Abbess chose;
A solemn hour, her secret to disclose.

XXI

"O holy Palmer!" she began—
"For sure he must be sainted man
  Whose blessèd feet have trod the ground
  Where the Redeemer's tomb is found—
  For His dear Church's sake my tale
  Attend, nor deem of light avail,
  Though I must speak of worldly love—
  How vain to those who wed above!
  De Wilton and Lord Marmion wooed
  Clara de Clare, of Gloucester's blood;
  Idle it were of Whitby's dame,

To say of that same blood I came;
And once, when jealous rage was high,
Lord Marmion said despiteously,
Wilton was traitor in his heart,
And had made league with Martin Swart,
When he came here on Simnel's part
And only cowardice did restrain
His rebel aid on Stokefield's plain,
And down he threw his glove: the thing
Was tried, as wont, before the king;
Where frankly did De Wilton own
That Swart in Gueldres he had known;
And that between them then there went
Some scroll of courteous compliment.
For this he to his castle sent;
But when his messenger returned,
Judge how De Wilton's fury burned
For in his packet there were laid
Letters that claimed disloyal aid,
And proved King Henry's cause betrayed.
His fame, thus blighted, in the field
He strove to clear by spear and shield;
To clear his fame in vain he strove,
For wondrous are His ways above!
Perchance some form was unobserved;
Perchance in prayer or faith he swerved;
Else how could guiltless champion quail,
Or how the blessèd ordeal fail?

XXII

"His squire, who now De Wilton saw
As recreant doomed to suffer law,
    Repentant, owned in vain,
That while he had the scrolls in care,
A stranger maiden, passing fair,
Had drenched him with a beverage rare;
    His words no faith could gain.
With Clare alone he credence won,

Who, rather than wed Marmion,
Did to Saint Hilda's shrine repair,
To give our house her livings fair,
And die a vestal vot'ress there.
The impulse from the earth was given,
But bent her to the paths of heaven.
A purer heart, a lovelier maid,
Ne'er sheltered her in Whitby's shade,
No, not since Saxon Edelfled:
     Only one trace of earthly strain,
          That for her lover's loss
     She cherishes a sorrow vain,
          And murmurs at the cross.
     And then her heritage;—it goes
          Along the banks of Tame;
     Deep fields of grain the reaper mows,
     In meadows rich the heifer lows,
     The falconer and huntsman knows
          Its woodlands for the game.
Shame were it to Saint Hilda dear,
And I, her humble vot'ress here,
     Should do a deadly sin,
Her temple spoiled before mine eyes,
If this false Marmion such a prize
     By my consent should win;
Yet hath our boisterous monarch sworn
That Clare shall from our house be torn;
And grievous cause have I to fear
Such mandate doth Lord Marmion bear.

XXIII

"Now, prisoner, helpless, and betrayed
To evil power, I claim thine aid,
     By every step that thou hast trod
To holy shrine and grotto dim,
By every martyr's tortured limb,
By angel, saint, and seraphim,
     And by the Church of God!

For mark:—When Wilton was betrayed,
And with his squire forged letters laid,
She was, alas! that sinful maid
    By whom the deed was done—
Oh! shame and horror to be said!—
    She was a perjured nun!
No clerk in all the land, like her
Traced quaint and varying character.
Perchance you may a marvel deem
    That Marmion's paramour
(For such vile thing she was) should scheme
    Her lover's nuptial hour;
But o'er him thus she hoped to gain,
As privy to his honour's stain,
    Illimitable power:
For this she secretly retained
    Each proof that might the plot reveal,
    Instructions with his hand and seal;
And thus Saint Hilda deigned,
      Through sinners' perfidy impure,
      Her house's glory to secure
    And Clare's immortal weal.

XXIV

"'Twere long and needless here to tell
How to my hand these papers fell;
    With me they must not stay.
Saint Hilda keep her Abbess true!
Who knows what outrage he might do
    While journeying by the way?
O blessèd saint, if e'er again
I venturous leave thy calm domain,
To travel or by land or main,
    Deep penance may I pay!
Now, saintly Palmer, mark my prayer:
I give this packet to thy care,
For thee to stop they will not dare;
    And, oh! with cautious speed

To Wolsey's hand the papers bring,
That he may show them to the king
 And for thy well-earned meed,
Thou holy man, at Whitby's shrine
A weekly mass shall still be thine
 While priests can sing and read.
What ail'st thou? Speak!" For as he took
The charge, a strong emotion shook
 His frame; and, ere reply,
They heard a faint yet shrilly tone,
Like distant clarion feebly blown,
 That on the breeze did die;
And loud the Abbess shrieked in fear,
"Saint Withold, save us! What is here?
 Look at yon city cross!
See, on its battled tower appear
Phantoms, that scutcheons seem to rear,
 And blazoned banners toss!"

XXV

Dunedin's Cross, a pillared stone,
Rose on a turret octagon;
(But now is razed that monument
 Whence royal edict rang,
And voice of Scotland's law was sent
 In glorious trumpet-clang.
Oh! be his tomb as lead to lead
Upon its dull destroyer's head!—
A minstrel's malison is said).
Then on its battlements they saw
A vision, passing Nature's law,
 Strange, wild, and dimly seen—
Figures that seemed to rise and die,
Gibber and sign, advance and fly,
While nought confirmed could ear or eye
 Discern of sound or mien.
Yet darkly did it seem, as there
Heralds and pursuivants prepare,

With trumpet sound and blazon fair,
 A summons to proclaim;
But indistinct the pageant proud,
As fancy-forms of midnight cloud,
When flings the moon upon her shroud
 A wavering tinge of flame;
It flits, expands, and shifts, till loud,
From midmost of the spectre crowd,
 This awful summons came:—

XXVI

"Prince, prelate, potentate, and peer,
 Whose names I now shall call,
Scottish, or foreigner, give ear!
Subjects of him who sent me here,
At his tribunal to appear
 I summon one and all:
I cite you by each deadly sin
That e'er hath soiled your hearts within;
I cite you by each brutal lust
That e'er defiled your earthly dust—
 By wrath, by pride, by fear;
By each o'er-mastering passion's tone,
By the dark grave and dying groan!
When forty days are passed and gone,
I cite you, at your monarch's throne,
 To answer and appear."
Then thundered forth a roll of names;
The first was thine, unhappy James!
 Then all thy nobles came:—
Crawford, Glencairn, Montrose, Argyle,
Ross, Bothwell, Forbes, Lennox, Lyle—
Why should I tell their separate style?
 Each chief of birth and fame,
Of Lowland, Highland, Border, Isle,
Foredoomed to Flodden's carnage pile,
 Was cited there by name;
And Marmion, Lord of Fontenaye,

Of Lutterward and Scrivelbaye;
De Wilton, erst of Aberley,
The self-same thundering voice did say.
    But then another spoke:
"Thy fatal summons I deny,
And thine infernal lord defy,
Appealing me to Him on high,
    Who burst the sinner's yoke."
At that dread accent, with a scream.
Parted the pageant like a dream,
    The summoner was gone.
Prone on her face the Abbess fell,
And fast and fast her beads did tell;
Her nuns came, startled by the yell,
    And found her there alone.
She marked not, at the scene aghast,
What time, or how, the Palmer passed.

XXVII

Shift we the scene. The camp doth move;
    Dunedin's streets are empty now,
Save when, for weal of those they love,
    To pray the prayer, and vow the vow,
The tottering child, the anxious fair,
The grey-haired sire, with pious care,
To chapels and to shrines repair—
Where is the Palmer now? and where
The Abbess, Marmion, and Clare?
Bold Douglas! to Tantallon fair
    They journey in thy charge.
Lord Marmion rode on his right hand,
The Palmer still was with the band;
Angus, like Lindesay, did command
    That none should roam at large.
But in that Palmer's altered mien
A wondrous change might now be seen;
    Freely he spoke of war,
Of marvels wrought by single hand

When lifted for a native land;
And still looked high, as if he planned
    Some desperate deed afar.
His courser would he feed and stroke,
And, tucking up his sable frock,
Would first his mettle bold provoke,
    Then soothe or quell his pride.
Old Hubert said, that never one
He saw, except Lord Marmion,
    A steed so fairly ride.

XXVIII

Some half-hour's march behind, there came,
    By Eustace governed fair,
A troop escorting Hilda's dame,
    With all her nuns and Clare.
No audience had Lord Marmion sought;
    Ever he feared to aggravate
    Clara de Clare's suspicious hate;
And safer 'twas, he thought,
    To wait till, from the nuns removed,
    The influence of kinsmen loved,
    And suit by Henry's self approved,
Her slow consent had wrought.
    His was no flickering flame, that dies
    Unless when fanned by looks and sighs,
    And lighted oft at lady's eyes;
    He longed to stretch his wide command
    O'er luckless Clara's ample land;
    Besides, when Wilton with him vied,
    Although the pang of humbled pride
    The place of jealousy supplied,
Yet conquest, by that meanness won
He almost loathed to think upon,
Led him, at times, to hate the cause
Which made him burst through honour's laws
If e'er he loved, 'twas her alone
Who died within that vault of stone.

And now when close at hand they saw
North Berwick's town and lofty Law,
Fitz-Eustace bade them pause awhile
Before a venerable pile,
    Whose turrets viewed, afar,
The lofty Bass, the Lambie Isle,
    The ocean's peace or war.
At tolling of a bell, forth came
The convent's venerable dame,
And prayed Saint Hilda's Abbess rest
With her, a loved and honoured guest,
Till Douglas should a barque prepare
To waft her back to Whitby fair.
Glad was the Abbess, you may guess,
And thanked the Scottish Prioress;
And tedious were to tell, I ween,
The courteous speech that passed between.
    O'erjoyed, the nuns their palfreys leave;
But when fair Clara did intend,
Like them, from horseback to descend,
    Fitz-Eustace said, "I grieve,
Fair lady—grieve e'en from my heart—
Such gentle company to part;
    Think not discourtesy,
But lords' commands must be obeyed;
And Marmion and the Douglas said
    That you must wend with me.
Lord Marmion hath a letter broad,
Which to the Scottish earl he showed,
Commanding that beneath his care
Without delay you shall repair
To your good kinsman, Lord Fitz-Clare."

XXX

The startled Abbess loud exclaimed;
But she at whom the blow was aimed

Grew pale as death, and cold as lead—
She deemed she heard her death-doom read.
"Cheer thee, my child," the Abbess said;
"They dare not tear thee from my hand
To ride alone with armèd band."

    "Nay, holy mother, nay,"
Fitz-Eustace said, "the lovely Clare
Will be in Lady Angus' care,
    In Scotland while we stay;
And when we move, an easy ride
Will bring us to the English side,
Female attendance to provide
    Befitting Gloucester's heir;
Nor thinks, nor dreams, my noble lord,
By slightest look, or act, or word,
    To harass Lady Clare.
Her faithful guardian he will be,
Nor sue for slightest courtesy
    That e'en to stranger falls.
Till he shall place her, safe and free,
    Within her kinsman's halls."
He spoke, and blushed with earnest grace;
His faith was painted on his face,
    And Clare's worst fear relieved.
The Lady Abbess loud exclaimed
On Henry, and the Douglas blamed,
    Entreated, threatened, grieved;
To martyr, saint, and prophet prayed,
Against Lord Marmion inveighed,
And called the Prioress to aid,
To curse with candle, bell, and book.
Her head the grave Cistercian shook:
"The Douglas and the King," she said,
"In their commands will be obeyed;
Grieve not, nor dream that harm can fall
The maiden in Tantallon Hall."

The Abbess, seeing strife was vain,
Assumed her wonted state again—
 For much of state she had—
Composed her veil, and raised her head,
And—"Bid," in solemn voice she said,
 "Thy master, bold and bad,
The records of his house turn o'er,
 And when he shall there written see,
 That one of his own ancestry
 Drove the monks forth of Coventry,
Bid him his fate explore.
 Prancing in pride of earthly trust,
 His charger hurled him to the dust,
 And, by a base plebeian thrust,
He died his band before.
 God judge 'twixt Marmion and me;
 He is a chief of high degree,
And I a poor recluse;
 Yet oft, in Holy Writ, we see
 Even such weak minister as me
May the oppressor bruise:
 For thus, inspired, did Judith slay
  The mighty in his sin,
 And Jael thus, and Deborah"—
  Here hasty Blount broke in:—
"Fitz-Eustace, we must march our band;
Saint Anton' fire thee! wilt thou stand
All day, with bonnet in thy hand,
 To hear the lady preach?
By this good light! if thus we stay,
Lord Marmion, for our fond delay,
 Will sharper sermon teach.
Come, don thy cap, and mount thy horse;
The dame must patience take perforce."

XXXII

"Submit we, then, to force," said Clare,
"But let this barbarous lord despair
    His purposed aim to win;
 Let him take living, land, and life;
 But to be Marmion's wedded wife
    In me were deadly sin:
And if it be the king's decree
That I must find no sanctuary
In that inviolable dome
Where even a homicide might come
    And safely rest his head,
Though at its open portals stood,
Thirsting to pour forth blood for blood,
    The kinsmen of the dead;
Yet one asylum is my own
    Against the dreaded hour—
A low, a silent, and a lone,
    Where kings have little power.
One victim is before me there.
Mother, your blessing, and in prayer
Remember your unhappy Clare!"
Loud weeps the Abbess, and bestows
    Kind blessings many a one:
Weeping and wailing loud arose
Round patient Clare, the clamorous woes
    Of every simple nun.
His eyes the gentle Eustace dried,
And scarce rude Blount the sight could bide.
    Then took the squire her rein,
And gently led away her steed,
And, by each courteous word and deed,
    To cheer her strove in vain.

XXXIII

But scant three miles the band had rode,
    When o'er a height they passed,

And, sudden, close before them showed
  His towers, Tantallon vast;
Broad, massive, high, and stretching far,
And held impregnable in war,
On a projecting rock they rose,
And round three sides the ocean flows,
The fourth did battled walls enclose,
  And double mound and fosse.
By narrow drawbridge, outworks strong,
Through studded gates, an entrance long,
  To the main court they cross;
It was a wide and stately square;
Around were lodgings, fit and fair,
  And towers of various form,
Which on the court projected far,
And broke its lines quadrangular.
Here was square keep, there turret high,
Or pinnacle that sought the sky,
Whence oft the warder could descry
  The gathering ocean-storm.

XXXIV

Here did they rest. The princely care
Of Douglas, why should I declare,
Or say they met reception fair?
  Or why the tidings say,
Which, varying, to Tantallon came,
By hurrying posts or fleeter fame,
  With every varying day?
And, first, they heard King James had won
  Etall, and Wark, and Ford; and then
  That Norham Castle strong was ta'en.
At that sore marvelled Marmion;
And Douglas hoped his monarch's hand
Would soon subdue Northumberland:
  But whispered news there came,
That, while his host inactive lay,
And melted by degrees away,

King James was dallying off the day
    With Heron's wily dame.
Such acts to chronicles I yield:
    Go seek them there and see;
Mine is a tale of Flodden Field,
    And not a history.
At length they heard the Scottish host
On that high ridge had made their post
    Which frowns o'er Milfield Plain,
And that brave Surrey many a band
Had gathered in the Southern land,
And marched into Northumberland,
    And camp at Wooler ta'en.
Marmion, like charger in the stall,
That hears, without, the trumpet call,
    Began to chafe and swear:
"A sorry thing to hide my head
In castle, like a fearful maid,
    When such a field is near!
Needs must I see this battle-day;
Death to my fame if such a fray
Were fought, and Marmion away!
The Douglas, too, I wot not why,
Hath 'bated of his courtesy:
No longer in his halls I'll stay."
Then bade his band they should array
For march against the dawning day.

Introduction to Canto Sixth

To Richard Heber, Esq.

—*Mertoun House, Christmas*

Heap on more wood! the wind is chill;
But let it whistle as it will,
We'll keep our Christmas merry still.
Each age has deemed the new-born year
The fittest time for festal cheer;
E'en, heathen yet, the savage Dane
At Iol more deep the mead did drain;
High on the beach his galleys drew,
And feasted all his pirate crew;
Then in his low and pine-built hall,
Where shields and axes decked the wall,
They gorged upon the half-dressed steer;
Caroused in seas of sable beer;
While round, in brutal jest, were thrown
The half-gnawed rib and marrow-bone;
Or listened all, in grim delight,
While scalds yelled out the joys of fight.
Then forth, in frenzy, would they hie,
While wildly-loose their red locks fly,
And dancing round the blazing pile,
They make such barbarous mirth the while,
As best might to the mind recall
The boist'rous joys of Odin's hall.

And well our Christian sires of old
Loved, when the year its course had rolled,
And brought blithe Christmas back again,
With all his hospitable train.
Domestic and religious rite
Gave honour to the holy night;
On Christmas Eve the bells were rung;
On Christmas Eve the mass was sung;
That only night in all the year

Saw the stoled priest the chalice rear.
The damsel donned her kirtle sheen;
The hall was dressed with holly green;
Forth to the wood did merry men go,
To gather in the mistletoe.
Then opened wide the baron's hall
To vassal, tenant, serf, and all;
Power laid his rod of rule aside,
And Ceremony doffed his pride.
The heir, with roses in his shoes,
That night might village partner choose;
The lord, underogating, share
The vulgar game of "post and pair."
All hailed, with uncontrolled delight,
And general voice, the happy night,
That to the cottage, as the crown,
Brought tidings of salvation down.

    The fire, with well-dried logs supplied,
Went roaring up the chimney wide;
The huge hall table's oaken face,
Scrubbed till it shone, the day to grace,
Bore then upon its massive board
No mark to part the squire and lord.
Then was brought in the lusty brawn,
By old blue-coated serving-man;
Then the grim boar's head frowned on high,
Crested with bays and rosemary.
Well can the green-garbed ranger tell,
How, when, and where, the monster fell:
What dogs before his death he tore,
And all the baiting of the boar.
The wassail round, in good brown bowls,
Garnished with ribbons, blithely trowls.
There the huge sirloin reeked; hard by
Plum-porridge stood, and Christmas pie;
Nor failed old Scotland to produce,
At such high tide, her savoury goose.
Then came the merry maskers in,
And carols roared with blithesome din;

If unmelodious was the song,
It was a hearty note, and strong.
Who lists may in their mumming see
Traces of ancient mystery;
White shirts supplied the masquerade,
And smutted cheeks the visors made;
But oh! what maskers richly dight
Can boast of bosoms half so light!
England was merry England, when
Old Christmas brought his sports again.
'Twas Christmas broached the mightiest ale;
'Twas Christmas told the merriest tale:
A Christmas gambol oft could cheer
The poor man's heart through half the year.

    Still linger, in our Northern clime,
Some remnants of the good old time;
And still, within our valleys here,
We hold the kindred title dear,
Even when, perchance, its far-fetched claim
To Southern ear sounds empty name;
For course of blood, our proverbs deem,
Is warmer than the mountain-stream.
And thus my Christmas still I hold
Where my great grandsire came of old,
With amber beard, and flaxen hair,
And reverend apostolic air—
The feast and holy-tide to share,
And mix sobriety with wine,
And honest mirth with thoughts divine:
Small thought was his in after time
E'er to be hitched into a rhyme.
The simple sire could only boast,
That he was loyal to his cost;
The banished race of kings revered,
And lost his land—but kept his beard.

    In these dear halls, where welcome kind
Is with fair liberty combined;
Where cordial friendship gives the hand,
And flies constraint the magic wand

Of the fair dame that rules the land.
Little we heed the tempest drear,
While music, mirth, and social cheer,
Speed on their wings the passing year.
And Mertoun's halls are fair e'en now,
When not a leaf is on the bough.
Tweed loves them well, and turns again,
As loth to leave the sweet domain,
And holds his mirror to her face,
And clips her with a close embrace:
Gladly as he, we seek the dome,
And as reluctant turn us home.

How just that, at this time of glee,
My thoughts should, Heber, turn to thee!
For many a merry hour we've known,
And heard the chimes of midnight's tone.
Cease, then, my friend! a moment cease,
And leave these classic tomes in peace!
Of Roman and of Grecian lore
Sure mortal brain can hold no more.
These ancients, as Noll Bluff might say,
"Were pretty fellows in their day;"
But time and tide o'er all prevail—
On Christmas eve a Christmas tale,
Of wonder and of war—"Profane!
What! leave the loftier Latian strain,
Her stately prose, her verse's charms,
To hear the clash of rusty arms:
In Fairy Land or Limbo lost,
To jostle conjuror and ghost,
Goblin and witch!" Nay, Heber dear,
Before you touch my charter, hear;
Though Leyden aids, alas! no more,
My cause with many-languaged lore,
This may I say:—in realms of death
Ulysses meets Alcides' *wraith*;
Æneas, upon Thracia's shore,
The ghost of murdered Polydore;
For omens, we in Livy cross,

At every turn, *locutus Bos*.
As grave and duly speaks that ox,
As if he told the price of stocks
Or held in Rome republican,
The place of common-councilman.

All nations have their omens drear,
Their legends wild of woe and fear.
To Cambria look—the peasant see
Bethink him of Glendowerdy,
And shun "the spirit's blasted tree."
The Highlander, whose red claymore
The battle turned on Maida's shore,
Will, on a Friday morn, look pale,
If asked to tell a fairy tale:
He fears the vengeful elfin king,
Who leaves that day his grassy ring:
Invisible to human ken,
He walks among the sons of men.

Did'st e'er, dear Heber, pass along
Beneath the towers of Franchèmont,
Which, like an eagle's nest in air,
Hang o'er the stream and hamlet fair;
Deep in their vaults, the peasants say,
A mighty treasure buried lay,
Amassed through rapine and through wrong,
By the last Lord of Franchèmont.
The iron chest is bolted hard,
A huntsman sits, its constant guard;
Around his neck his horn is hung,
His hanger in his belt is slung;
Before his feet his blood-hounds lie:
And 'twere not for his gloomy eye,
Whose withering glance no heart can brook,
As true a huntsman doth he look,
As bugle e'er in brake did sound,
Or ever hallooed to a hound.
To chase the fiend, and win the prize,
In that same dungeon ever tries
An aged necromantic priest:

It is an hundred years at least,
Since 'twixt them first the strife begun,
And neither yet has lost nor won.
And oft the conjuror's words will make
The stubborn demon groan and quake;
And oft the bands of iron break,
Or bursts one lock, that still amain,
Fast as 'tis opened, shuts again.
That magic strife within the tomb
May last until the day of doom,
Unless the adept shall learn to tell
The very word that clenched the spell,
When Franchèmont locked the treasure cell.
A hundred years are past and gone,
And scarce three letters has he won.

    Such general superstition may
Excuse for old Pitscottie say;
Whose gossip history has given
My song the messenger from heaven,
That warned, in Lithgow, Scotland's king,
Nor less the infernal summoning;
May pass the monk of Durham's tale,
Whose demon fought in Gothic mail;
May pardon plead for Fordun grave,
Who told of Gifford's goblin-cave.
But why such instances to you,
Who in an instant can renew
Your treasured hoards of various lore,
And furnish twenty thousand more?
Hoards, not like theirs whose volumes rest
Like treasures in the Franchèmont chest,
While gripple owners still refuse
To others what they cannot use;
Give them the priest's whole century,
They shall not spell you letters three;
Their pleasure in the books the same
The magpie takes in pilfered gem.
Thy volumes, open as thy heart,
Delight, amusement, science, art,

To every ear and eye impart;
Yet who, of all who thus employ them,
Can like the owner's self enjoy them?
But, hark! I hear the distant drum!
The day of Flodden Field is come.
Adieu, dear Heber! life and health,
And store of literary wealth!

Canto Sixth

THE BATTLE

I

WHILE great events were on the gale,
And each hour brought a varying tale,
And the demeanour, changed and cold,
Of Douglas fretted Marmion bold,
And, like the impatient steed of war
He snuffed the battle from afar;
And hopes were none, that back again
Herald should come from Terouenne,
Where England's king in leaguer lay,
Before decisive battle-day;
Whilst these things were, the mournful Clare
Did in the dame's devotions share:
For the good countess ceaseless prayed
To Heaven and saints, her sons to aid,
And with short interval did pass
From prayer to book, from book to mass,
And all in high baronial pride—
A life both dull and dignified;
Yet as Lord Marmion nothing pressed
Upon her intervals of rest,
Dejected Clara well could bear
The formal state, the lengthened prayer,
Though dearest to her wounded heart
The hours that she might spend apart.

II

I said, Tantallon's dizzy steep
Hung o'er the margin of the deep.
Many a rude tower and rampart there
Repelled the insult of the air,

Which, when the tempest vexed the sky,
Half breeze, half spray, came whistling by.
Above the rest, a turret square
Did o'er its Gothic entrance bear,
Of sculpture rude, a stony shield;
The bloody heart was in the field,
And in the chief three mullets stood,
The cognisance of Douglas blood.
The turret held a narrow stair,
Which, mounted, gave you access where
A parapet's embattled row
Did seaward round the castle go.
Sometimes in dizzy steps descending,
Sometimes in narrow circuit bending,
Sometimes in platform broad extending,
Its varying circle did combine
Bulwark, and bartisan, and line,
And bastion, tower, and vantage-coign:
Above the booming ocean leant
The far projecting battlement;
The billows burst in ceaseless flow
Upon the precipice below.
Where'er Tantallon faced the land,
Gateworks and walls were strongly manned;
No need upon the sea-girt side;
The steepy rock, and frantic tide,
Approach of human step denied;
And thus these lines, and ramparts rude,
Were left in deepest solitude.

III

And, for they were so lonely, Clare
Would to these battlements repair,
And muse upon her sorrows there,
    And list the sea-bird's cry;
Or slow, like noontide ghost, would glide
Along the dark grey bulwark's side,

And ever on the heaving tide
 Look down with weary eye.
Oft did the cliff, and swelling main,
Recall the thoughts of Whitby's fane—
A home she ne'er might see again;
 For she had laid adown,
So Douglas bade, the hood and veil,
And frontlet of the cloister pale,
 And Benedictine gown:
It were unseemly sight, he said,
A novice out of convent shade.
Now her bright locks, with sunny glow,
Again adorned her brow of snow;
Her mantle rich, whose borders round,
A deep and fretted broidery bound,
In golden foldings sought the ground;
Of holy ornament, alone
Remained a cross with ruby stone;
 And often did she look
On that which in her hand she bore,
With velvet bound, and broidered o'er,
 Her breviary book.
In such a place, so lone, so grim,
At dawning pale, or twilight dim,
 It fearful would have been
To meet a form so richly dressed,
With book in hand, and cross on breast,
 And such a woeful mien.
Fitz-Eustace, loitering with his bow,
To practise on the gull and crow,
Saw her, at distance, gliding slow,
 And did by Mary swear—
Some lovelorn fay she might have been,
Or, in romance, some spell-bound queen;
For ne'er, in work-day world, was seen
 A form so witching fair.

Once walking thus, at evening tide,
It chanced a gliding sail she spied,
And, sighing, thought—"The Abbess, there,
Perchance, does to her home repair;
Her peaceful rule, where Duty, free,
Walks hand in hand with Charity;
Where oft Devotion's trancèd glow
Can such a glimpse of heaven bestow,
That the enraptured sisters see
High vision, and deep mystery;
The very form of Hilda fair,
Hovering upon the sunny air,
And smiling on her votaries' prayer.
Oh! wherefore, to my duller eye,
Did still the saint her form deny!
Was it that, seared by sinful scorn,
My heart could neither melt nor burn?
Or lie my warm affections low,
With him, that taught them first to glow?
Yet, gentle Abbess, well I knew,
To pay thy kindness grateful due,
And well could brook the mild command,
That ruled thy simple maiden band.
How different now! condemned to bide
My doom from this dark tyrant's pride.
But Marmion has to learn, ere long,
That constant mind, and hate of wrong,
Descended to a feeble girl,
From Red De Clare, stout Gloucester's Earl:
Of such a stem, a sapling weak,
He ne'er shall bend, although he break."

V

"But see;—what makes this armour here?"
    For in her path there lay
  Targe, corslet, helm;—she viewed them near.

"The breast-plate pierced!—Ay, much I fear,
Weak fence wert thou 'gainst foeman's spear,
That hath made fatal entrance here,
    As these dark blood-gouts say.
Thus, Wilton! Oh! not corslet's ward,
Not truth, as diamond pure and hard,
Could be thy manly bosom's guard,
    On yon disastrous day!"
She raised her eyes in mournful mood—
Wilton himself before her stood!
It might have seemed his passing ghost,
For every youthful grace was lost;
And joy unwonted, and surprise,
Gave their strange wildness to his eyes.
Expect not, noble dames and lords,
That I can tell such scene in words:
What skilful limner e'er would choose
To paint the rainbow's varying hues,
Unless to mortal it were given
To dip his brush in dyes of heaven?
Far less can my weak line declare
    Each changing passion's shade:
Bright'ning to rapture from despair,
Sorrow, surprise, and pity there,
And joy, with her angelic air,
And hope, that paints the future fair,
    Their varying hues displayed:
Each o'er its rival's ground extending,
Alternate conquering, shifting, blending.
Till all, fatigued, the conflict yield,
And mighty Love retains the field.
Shortly I tell what then he said,
By many a tender word delayed,
And modest blush, and bursting sigh,
And question kind, and fond reply:—

DE WILTON'S HISTORY

"Forget we that disastrous day,
When senseless in the lists I lay.
    Thence dragged—but how I cannot know,
       For, sense and recollection fled,
    I found me on a pallet low,
       Within my ancient beadsman's shed.
    Austin—remember'st thou, my Clare,
How thou didst blush, when the old man,
When first our infant love began,
    Said we would make a matchless pair?
Menials and friends and kinsmen fled
From the degraded traitor's bed—
He only held my burning head,
And tended me for many a day,
While wounds and fever held their sway
But far more needful was his care,
When sense returned to wake despair;
    For I did tear the closing wound,
    And dash me frantic on the ground,
If e'er I heard the name of Clare.
At length, to calmer reason brought,
Much by his kind attendance wrought,
    With him I left my native strand,
And, in a palmer's weeds arrayed.
My hated name and form to shade
    I journeyed many a land;
No more a lord of rank and birth,
But mingled with the dregs of earth.
    Oft Austin for my reason feared,
When I would sit, and deeply brood
On dark revenge, and deeds of blood,
    Or wild mad schemes upreared.
My friend at length fell sick, and said,
    God would remove him soon:
And, while upon his dying bed,

He begged of me a boon—
If e'er my deadliest enemy
Beneath my brand should conquered lie,
Even then my mercy should awake,
And spare his life for Austin's sake.

VII

"Still restless as a second Cain,
To Scotland next my route was ta'en,
    Full well the paths I knew.
Fame of my fate made various sound,
That death in pilgrimage I found,
That I had perished of my wound—
    None cared which tale was true:
And living eye could never guess
De Wilton in his palmer's dress;
For now that sable slough is shed,
And trimmed my shaggy beard and head,
I scarcely know me in the glass.
A chance most wondrous did provide
That I should be that baron's guide—
    I will not name his name!—
Vengeance to God alone belongs;
But when I think on all my wrongs,
    My blood is liquid flame!
And ne'er the time shall I forget,
When, in a Scottish hostel set,
    Dark looks we did exchange:
What were his thoughts I cannot tell;
But in my bosom mustered Hell
    Its plans of dark revenge.

VIII

"A word of vulgar augury,
That broke from me, I scarce knew why,
    Brought on a village tale;
Which wrought upon his moody sprite,

And sent him arméd forth by night.
    I borrowed steed and mail,
And weapons, from his sleeping band;
And, passing from a postern door,
We met, and countered hand to hand—
    He fell on Gifford Moor.
For the death-stroke my brand I drew—
Oh, then my helmdd head he knew,
    The palmer's cowl was gone—
Then had three inches of my blade
The heavy debt of vengeance paid—
My hand the thought of Austin stayed;
    I left him there alone.
O good old man! even from the grave,
Thy spirit could thy master save:
If I had slain my foeman, ne'er
Had Whitby's Abbess, in her fear,
Given to my hand this packet dear,
Of power to clear my injured fame,
And vindicate De Wilton's name.
Perchance you heard the Abbess tell
Of the strange pageantry of Hell,
    That broke our secret speech—
It rose from the infernal shade,
Or featly was some juggle played,
    A tale of peace to teach.
Appeal to Heaven I judged was best,
When my name came among the rest.

IX

"Now here, within Tantallon Hold,
To Douglas late my tale I told,
To whom my house was known of old.
Won by my proofs, his falchion bright
This eve anew shall dub me knight.
These were the arms that once did turn
The tide of fight on Otterburne,
And Harry Hotspur forced to yield,

When the dead Douglas won the field.
These Angus gave—his armourer's care,
Ere morn, shall every breach repair;
For naught, he said, was in his halls,
But ancient armour on the walls,
And aged chargers in the stalls,
And women, priests, and grey-haired men;
The rest were all in Twisel Glen.
And now I watch my armour here,
By law of arms, till midnight's near;
Then, once again a belted knight,
Seek Surrey's camp with dawn of light.

X

"There soon again we meet, my Clare!
This baron means to guide thee there;
Douglas reveres his king's command,
Else would he take thee from his band
And there thy kinsman Surrey, too,
Will give De Wilton justice due.
Now meeter far for martial broil,
Firmer my limbs, and strung by toil,
Once more"—"O Wilton! must we then
Risk new-found happiness again,
    Trust fate of arms once more?
And is there not an humble glen,
    Where we, content and poor,
Might build a cottage in the shade,
A shepherd thou, and I to aid
    Thy task on dale and moor?—
That reddening brow!—too well I know,
Not even thy Clare can peace bestow,
    While falsehood stains thy name:
Go, then, to fight! Clare bids thee go!
Clare can a warrior's feelings know,
    And weep a warrior's shame;
Can Red Earl Gilbert's spirit feel,
Buckle the spurs upon thy heel,

And belt thee with thy brand of steel,
    And send thee forth to fame!"

XI

That night, upon the rocks and bay,
The midnight moonbeam slumbering lay,
And poured its silver light, and pure,
Through loophole, and through embrazure,
    Upon Tantallon's tower and hall;
But chief where archéd windows wide
Illuminate the chapel's pride,
    The sober glances fall.
Much was there need; though, seamed with scars,
Two veterans of the Douglas' wars,
    Though two grey priests were there,
And each a blazing torch held high,
You could not by their blaze descry
    The chapel's carving fair.
Amid that dim and smoky light,
Chequering the silvery moonshine bright,
    A bishop by the altar stood,
    A noble lord of Douglas blood,
With mitre sheen, and rocquet white.
Yet showed his meek and thoughtful eye
But little pride of prelacy;
More pleased that, in a barbarous age,
He gave rude Scotland Virgil's page,
Than that beneath his rule he held
The bishopric of fair Dunkeld.
Beside him ancient Angus stood,
Doffed his furred gown, and sable hood:
O'er his huge form and visage pale
He wore a cap and shirt of mail;
And leaned his large and wrinkled hand
Upon the huge and sweeping brand
Which wont of yore, in battle fray,
His foeman's limbs to shred away,
As wood-knife lops the sapling spray.

He seemed as, from the tombs around
 Rising at Judgment-Day,
 Some giant Douglas may be found
  In all his old array;
So pale his face, so huge his limb,
So old his arms, his look so grim.

XII

Then at the altar Wilton kneels,
And Clare the spurs bound on his heels;
And think what next he must have felt
At buckling of the falchion belt!
 And judge how Clara changed her hue,
While fastening to her lover's side
A friend, which, though in danger tried,
 He once had found untrue!
Then Douglas struck him with his blade:
"Saint Michael and Saint Andrew aid,
  I dub thee knight.
Arise, Sir Ralph, De Wilton's heir!
For king, for church, for lady fair,
  See that thou fight."
And Bishop Gawain, as he rose,
Said—"Wilton! grieve not for thy woes,
 Disgrace, and trouble;
For he, who honour best bestows,
 May give thee double."
De Wilton sobbed, for sob he must—
"Where'er I meet a Douglas, trust
 That Douglas is my brother!"
"Nay, nay," old Douglas said, "not so;
To Surrey's camp thou now must go,
 Thy wrongs no longer smother.
I have two sons in yonder field;
And, if thou meet'st them under shield
Upon them bravely—do thy worst;
And foul fall him that blenches first!"

XIII

Not far advanced was morning day,
When Marmion did his troop array,
    To Surrey's camp to ride;
He had safe-conduct for his band,
Beneath the royal seal and hand,
    And Douglas gave a guide:
The ancient earl, with stately grace,
Would Clara on her palfrey place,
And whispered in an under-tone,
"Let the hawk stoop, his prey is flown."
The train from out the castle drew,
But Marmion stopped to bid adieu:—
"Though something I might plain," he said,
"Of cold respect to stranger guest,
Sent hither by your king's behest,
    While in Tantallon's towers I stayed;
Part we in friendship from your land,
And, noble earl, receive my hand."
But Douglas round him drew his cloak,
Folded his arms, and thus he spoke:
"My manors, halls, and bowers, shall still
Be open, at my sovereign's will,
To each one whom he lists, howe'er
Unmeet to be the owner's peer.
My castles are my king's alone,
From turret to foundation-stone—
The hand of Douglas is his own;
And never shall in friendly grasp
The hand of such as Marmion clasp."

XIV

Burned Marmion's swarthy cheek like fire,
And shook his very frame for ire,
    And—"This to me!" he said;
"'An 'twere not for thy hoary head,
Such hand as Marmion's had not spared

SIR WALTER SCOTT

To cleave the Douglas' head!
And, first, I tell thee, haughty peer,
He who does England's message here,
Although the meanest in her state,
May well, proud Angus, be thy mate:
And, Douglas, more I tell thee here,
    Even in thy pitch of pride,
Here in thy hold, thy vassals near—
Nay, never look upon your lord,
And lay your hands upon your sword—
    I tell thee, thou'rt defied!
And if thou said'st, I am not peer
To any lord in Scotland here,
Lowland or Highland, far or near,
    Lord Angus, thou hast lied!"
On the Earl's cheek the flush of rage
O'ercame the ashen hue of age:
Fierce he broke forth—"And dar'st thou then
To beard the lion in his den,
    The Douglas in his hall?
And hop'st thou thence unscathed to go:
No, by Saint Bride of Bothwell, no!
Up drawbridge, grooms—what, warder, ho
    Let the portcullis fall."
Lord Marmion turned—well was his need,
And dashed the rowels in his steed,
Like arrow through the archway sprung,
The ponderous gate behind him rung:
To pass there was such scanty room,
The bars descending razed his plume.

XV

The steed along the drawbridge flies,
Just as it trembled on the rise;
Nor lighter does the swallow skim
Along the smooth lake's level brim:
And when Lord Marmion reached his band,
He halts, and turns with clenchéd hand,

And shout of loud defiance pours,
And shook his gauntlet at the towers.
"Horse! horse!" the Douglas cried, "and chase!"
But soon he reined his fury's pace:
"A royal messenger he came,
Though most unworthy of the name.
A letter forged! Saint Jude to speed!
Did ever knight so foul a deed!
At first in heart it liked me ill,
When the King praised his clerkly skill.
Thanks to St. Bothan, son of mine,
Save Gawain, ne'er could pen a line:
So swore I, and I swear it still,
Let my boy-bishop fret his fill.
Saint Mary mend my fiery mood!
Old age ne'er cools the Douglas blood,
I thought to slay him where he stood.
'Tis pity of him, too," he cried:
"Bold can he speak, and fairly ride,
I warrant him a warrior tried."
With this his mandate he recalls,
And slowly seeks his castle halls.

XVI

The day in Marmion's journey wore;
Yet, ere his passion's gust was o'er,
They crossed the heights of Stanrig Moor.
His troop more closely there he scanned,
And missed the Palmer from the band.
"Palmer or not," young Blount did say,
"He parted at the peep of day;
Good sooth it was in strange array."
"In what array?" said Marmion, quick.
"My lord, I ill can spell the trick;
But all night long, with clink and bang,
Close to my couch did hammers clang;
At dawn the falling drawbridge rang,
And from a loophole while I peep,

Old Bell-the-Cat came from the keep,
Wrapped in a gown of sables fair,
As fearful of the morning air;
Beneath, when that was blown aside,
A rusty shirt of mail I spied,
By Archibald won in bloody work
Against the Saracen and Turk:
Last night it hung not in the hall;
I thought some marvel would befall.
And next I saw them saddled lead
Old Cheviot forth, the earl's best steed;
A matchless horse, though something old,
Prompt in his paces, cool, and bold.
I heard the sheriff Sholto say,
The earl did much the master pray
To use him on the battle-day;
But he preferred"—"Nay, Henry, cease
Thou sworn horse-courser, hold thy peace.
Eustace, thou bear'st a brain—I pray
What did Blount see at break of day?"

XVII

"In brief, my lord, we both descried
(For then I stood by Henry's side)
The Palmer mount, and outwards ride,
    Upon the earl's own favourite steed:
All sheathed he was in armour bright,
And much resembled that same knight,
Subdued by you in Cotswold fight:
    Lord Angus wished him speed."
The instant that Fitz-Eustace spoke,
A sudden light on Marmion broke:
"Ah! dastard fool, to reason lost!"
He muttered; "'Twas nor fay nor ghost
I met upon the moonlight wold,
But living man of earthly mould.
    O dotage blind and gross!
Had I but fought as wont, one thrust

Had laid De Wilton in the dust,
    My path no more to cross.
How stand we now?—he told his tale
To Douglas; and with some avail;
    'Twas therefore gloomed his ruggéd brow.
Will Surrey dare to entertain,
'Gainst Marmion, charge disproved and vain?
    Small risk of that, I trow.
Yet Clare's sharp questions must I shun;
Must separate Constance from the nun—
Oh, what a tangled web we weave,
When first we practise to deceive!
A Palmer too!—no wonder why
I felt rebuked beneath his eye:
I might have known there was but one
Whose look could quell Lord Marmion."

XVIII

Stung with these thoughts, he urged to speed
His troop, and reached, at eve, the Tweed,
Where Lennel's convent closed their march;
(There now is left but one frail arch,
    Yet mourn thou not its cells:
Our time a fair exchange has made;
Hard by, in hospitable shade,
    A reverend pilgrim dwells,
Well worth the whole Bernardine brood
That e'er wore sandal, frock, or hood.)
Yet did Saint Bernard's Abbot there
Give Marmion entertainment fair,
And lodging for his train and Clare.
Next morn the baron climbed the tower,
To view afar the Scottish power,
    Encamped on Flodden edge:
The white pavilions made a show,
Like remnants of the winter snow,
    Along the dusky ridge.
Long Marmion looked: at length his eye

Unusual movement might descry
    Amid the shifting lines:
The Scottish host drawn out appears,
For, flashing on the edge of spears
    The eastern sunbeam shines.
Their front now deepening, now extending
Their flank inclining, wheeling, bending,
Now drawing back, and now descending,
The skilful Marmion well could know,
They watched the motions of some foe,
Who traversed on the plain below.

XIX

Even so it was. From Flodden ridge
    The Scots beheld the English host
    Leave Barmore Wood, their evening post,
    And heedful watched them as they crossed
The Till by Twisel Bridge.
    High sight it is, and haughty, while
    They dive into the deep defile;
    Beneath the caverned cliff they fall,
    Beneath the castle's airy wall.
By rock, by oak, by hawthorn tree,
    Troop after troop are disappearing;
    Troop after troop their banners rearing;
Upon the eastern bank you see.
Still pouring down the rocky den,
    Where flows the sullen Till,
And rising from the dim-wood glen,
Standards on stardards, men on men,
    In slow succession still,
And, sweeping o'er the Gothic arch,
And pressing on, in ceaseless march,
    To gain the opposing hill.
That morn, to many a trumpet clang,
Twisel! thy rocks deep echo rang;
And many a chief of birth and rank,
Saint Helen! at thy fountain drank.

Thy hawthorn glade which now we see
In spring-tide bloom so lavishly,
Had then from many an axe its doom,
To give the marching columns room.

XX

And why stands Scotland idly now,
Dark Flodden! on thy airy brow,
Since England gains the pass the while,
And struggles through the deep defile?
What checks the fiery soul of James?
Why sits that champion of the dames
 Inactive on his steed,
And sees, between him and his land,
Between him and Tweed's southern strand,
 His host Lord Surrey lead?
What 'vails the vain knight-errant's brand?
Oh, Douglas for thy leading wand!
 Fierce Randolph, for thy speed!
Oh, for one hour of Wallace wight,
Or well-skilled Bruce, to rule the fight,
And cry, "Saint Andrew and our right!"
Another sight had seen that morn,
From Fate's dark book a leaf been torn,
And Flodden had been Bannockbourne!
The precious hour has passed in vain,
And England's host has gained the plain;
Wheeling their march, and circling still,
Around the base of Flodden Hill.

XXI

Ere yet the bands met Marmion's eye,
Fitz-Eustace shouted loud and high,
"Hark! hark! my lord, an English drum!
And see ascending squadrons come
 Between Tweed's river and the hill,
Foot, horse, and cannon: hap what hap,

My basnet to a 'prentice cap,
    Lord Surrey's o'er the Till!
Yet more! yet more!—how far arrayed
They file from out the hawthorn shade,
    And sweep so gallant by!
With all their banners bravely spread,
    And all their armour flashing high,
Saint George might waken from the dead,
    To see fair England's standards fly."
"Stint in thy prate," quoth Blount, "thou'dst best,
And listen to our lord's behest."
With kindling brow Lord Marmion said—
"This instant be our band arrayed;
The river must be quickly crossed,
That we may join Lord Surrey's host.
If fight King James—as well I trust
That fight he will, and fight he must,
The Lady Clare behind our lines
Shall tarry, while the battle joins."

XXII

Himself he swift on horseback threw,
Scarce to the Abbot bade adieu;
Far less would listen to his prayer,
To leave behind the helpless Clare.
Down to the Tweed his band he drew,
And muttered, as the flood they view,
"The pheasant in the falcon's claw,
He scarce will yield to please a daw:
Lord Angus may the Abbot awe,
    So Clare shall bide with me."
Then on that dangerous ford, and deep,
Where to the Tweed Leat's eddies creep,
    He ventured desperately:
And not a moment will he bide,
Till squire, or groom, before him ride;
Headmost of all he stems the tide,
    And stems it gallantly.

Eustace held Clare upon her horse,
    Old Hubert led her rein,
Stoutly they braved the current's course,
And though far downward driven per force,
    The southern bank they gain;
Behind them straggling, came to shore,
    As best they might, the train;
Each o'er his head his yew-bow bore,
    A caution not in vain;
Deep need that day that every string,
By wet unharmed, should sharply ring.
A moment then Lord Marmion stayed,
And breathed his steed, his men arrayed,
    Then forward moved his band,
Until, Lord Surrey's rear-guard won,
He halted by a cross of stone,
That, on a hillock standing lone,
    Did all the field command.

XXIII

Hence might they see the full array
Of either host, for deadly fray;
Their marshalled lines stretched east and west,
    And fronted north and south,
And distant salutation passed
    From the loud cannon mouth;
Not in the close successive rattle,
That breathes the voice of modern battle,
    But slow and far between.
The hillock gained, Lord Marmion stayed:
"Here, by this cross," he gently said,
"You well may view the scene.
 Here shalt thou tarry, lovely Clare:
 Oh! think of Marmion in thy prayer!
 Thou wilt not? well—no less my care
 Shall, watchful, for thy weal prepare.
 You, Blount and Eustace, are her guard,
    With ten picked archers of my train;

With England if the day go hard,
    To Berwick speed amain.
But if we conquer, cruel maid,
My spoils shall at your feet be laid,
    When here we meet again."
He waited not for answer there,
And would not mark the maid's despair,
    Nor heed the discontented look
From either squire; but spurred amain,
And, dashing through the battle plain,
    His way to Surrey took.

XXIV

"The good Lord Marmion, by my life!
    Welcome to danger's hour!
Short greeting serves in time of strife:
    Thus have I ranged my power:
Myself will rule this central host,
    Stout Stanley fronts their right,
My sons command the vaward post,
    With Brian Tunstall, stainless knight:
    Lord Dacre, with his horsemen light,
    Shall be in rearward of the fight,
And succour those that need it most.
    Now, gallant Marmion, well I know,
    Would gladly to the vanguard go;
Edmund, the Admiral, Tunstall there,
With thee their charge will blithely share:
There fight thine own retainers too,
Beneath De Burg, thy steward true."
"Thanks, noble Surrey!" Marmion said,
Nor farther greeting there he paid;
But, parting like a thunderbolt,
First in the vanguard made a halt,
    Where such a shout there rose
Of "Marmion! Marmion!" that the cry
Up Flodden mountain shrilling high,
    Startled the Scottish foes.

Blount and Fitz-Eustace rested still
With Lady Clare upon the hill;
On which, for far the day was spent,
The western sunbeams now were bent.
The cry they heard, its meaning knew,
Could plain their distant comrades view:
Sadly to Blount did Eustace say,
"Unworthy office here to stay!
No hope of gilded spurs to-day.
But see! look up—on Flodden bent
The Scottish foe has fired his tent."
     And sudden, as he spoke,
From the sharp ridges of the hill,
All downward to the banks of Till,
     Was wreathed in sable smoke.
Volumed and fast, and rolling far,
The cloud enveloped Scotland's war,
     As down the hill they broke;
Nor martial shout, nor minstrel tone,
Announced their march; their tread alone
At times one warning trumpet blown,
     At times a stifled hum,
Told England, from his mountain-throne
     King James did rushing come.
Scarce could they hear or see their foes,
     Until at weapon-point they close.
They close, in clouds of smoke and dust,
With sword-sway, and with lance's thrust;
     And such a yell was there,
Of sudden and portentous birth,
As if men fought upon the earth,
     And fiends in upper air;
Oh, life and death were in the shout,
Recoil and rally, charge and rout,
     And triumph and despair.
Long looked the anxious squires; their eye
Could in the darkness nought descry.

XXVI

At length the freshening western blast
Aside the shroud of battle cast;
And, first, the ridge of mingled spears
Above the brightening cloud appears;
And in the smoke the pennons flew,
As in the storm the white sea-mew.
Then marked they, dashing broad and far,
The broken billows of the war,
And plumèd crests of chieftains brave
Floating like foam upon the wave;
    But nought distinct they see:
Wide raged the battle on the plain;
Spears shook, and falchions flashed amain;
Fell England's arrow-flight like rain;
Crests rose, and stooped, and rose again,
    Wild and disorderly.
Amid the scene of tumult, high
They saw Lord Marmion's falcon fly:
And stainless Tunstall's banner white,
And Edmund Howard's lion bright,
Still bear them bravely in the fight;
    Although against them come,
Of gallant Gordons many a one,
And many a stubborn Badenoch-man,
And many a rugged Border clan,
    With Huntley and with Home.

XXVII

Far on the left, unseen the while,
Stanley broke Lennox and Argyle;
Though there the western mountaineer
Rushed with bare bosom on the spear,
And flung the feeble targe aside,
And with both hands the broadsword plied,
'Twas vain:—But Fortune, on the right,
With fickle smile, cheered Scotland's fight.

Then fell that spotless banner white,
    The Howard's lion fell;
Yet still Lord Marmion's falcon flew
With wavering flight, while fiercer grew
    Around the battle-yell.
The Border slogan rent the sky!
A Home! a Gordon! was the cry:
Loud were the clanging blows;
Advanced—forced back—now low, now high,
    The pennon sunk and rose;
As bends the barque's mast in the gale,
When rent are rigging, shrouds, and sail,
    It wavered 'mid the foes.
No longer Blount the view could bear:
"By heaven and all its saints! I swear,
    I will not see it lost;
Fitz-Eustace, you with Lady Clare
May bid your beads, and patter prayer—
    I gallop to the host."
And to the fray he rode amain,
Followed by all the archer train.
The fiery youth, with desperate charge,
Made, for a space, an opening large—
    The rescued banner rose—
But darkly closed the war around,
Like pine-trees, rooted from the ground,
    It sunk among the foes.
Then Eustace mounted too:—yet stayed,
As loth to leave the helpless maid,
    When, fast as shaft can fly,
Bloodshot his eyes, his nostrils spread,
The loose rein dangling from his head,
Housing and saddle bloody red,
    Lord Marmion's steed rushed by;
And Eustace, maddening at the sight,
    A look and sign to Clara cast,
    To mark he would return in haste,
Then plunged into the fight.

XXVIII

Ask me not what the maiden feels,
    Left in that dreadful hour alone:
Perchance her reason stoops or reels;
    Perchance a courage not her own,
    Braces her mind to desperate tone.
The scattered van of England wheels;
    She only said, as loud in air
    The tumult roared, "Is Wilton there?"
    They fly, or, maddened by despair,
Fight but to die—"Is Wilton there?"
With that, straight up the hill there rode
    Two horsemen drenched with gore,
And in their arms, a helpless load,
    A wounded knight they bore.
His hand still strained the broken brand;
His arms were smeared with blood and sand.
Dragged from among the horses' feet,
With dinted shield and helmet beat,
The falcon-crest and plumage gone,
Can that be haughty Marmion? . . .
Young Blount his armour did unlace,
And, gazing on his ghastly face,
    Said—"By Saint George, he's gone!
That spear-wound has our master sped—
And see, the deep cut on his head!
    Good-night to Marmion."
"Unnurtured Blount! thy brawling cease:
He opes his eyes," said Eustace; "peace!"

XXIX

When, doffed his casque, he felt free air,
Around 'gan Marmion wildly stare:—
"Where's Harry Blount? Fitz-Eustace where?
Linger ye here, ye hearts of hare?
Redeem my pennon—charge again!
Cry—'Marmion to the rescue!'—Vain!

Last of my race, on battle-plain
That shout shall ne'er be heard again!
Yet my last thought is England's—fly,
 To Dacre bear my signet ring:
 Tell him his squadrons up to bring.
Fitz-Eustace, to Lord Surrey hie;
 Tunstall lies dead upon the field,
 His life-blood stains the spotless shield
 Edmund is down:—my life is reft;
 The Admiral alone is left.
 Let Stanley charge with spur of fire—
 With Chester charge, and Lancashire,
 Full upon Scotland's central host,
 Or victory and England's lost.
 Must I bid twice?—hence, varlets! fly!
 Leave Marmion here alone—to die."
 They parted, and alone he lay;
 Clare drew her from the sight away,
Till pain rung forth a lowly moan,
And half he murmured—"Is there none,
 Of all my halls have nursed,
Page, squire, or groom, one cup to bring
Of blessèd water from the spring,
 To slake my dying thirst?"

XXX

O woman! in our hours of ease,
Uncertain, coy, and hard to please,
And variable as the shade
By the light quivering aspen made;
When pain and anguish wring the brow,
A ministering angel thou!
Scarce were the piteous accents said,
When, with the baron's casque, the maid
 To the nigh streamlet ran:
Forgot were hatred, wrongs, and fears;
The plaintive voice alone she hears,
 Sees but the dying man.

She stooped her by the runnel's side,
　　But in abhorrence backward drew;
For, oozing from the mountain's side,
Where raged the war, a dark-red tide
　　Was curdling in the streamlet blue.
Where shall she turn?—behold her mark
　　A little fountain cell,
Where water, clear as diamond-spark,
　　In a stone basin fell.
Above some half-worn letters say,
"Drink, weary pilgrim, drink and pray
For the kind soul of Sybil Gray,
　　Who built this cross and well."
She filled the helm, and back she hied,
And with surprise and joy espied
　　A monk supporting Marmion's head;
A pious man, whom duty brought
To dubious verge of battle fought,
　　To shrive the dying, bless the dead.

XXXI

Deep drank Lord Marmion of the wave,
And, as she stooped his brow to lave—
"Is it the hand of Clare," he said,
"Or injured Constance, bathes my head?"
　　Then, as remembrance rose—
"Speak not to me of shrift or prayer!
　　I must redress her woes.
Short space, few words, are mine to spare;
Forgive and listen, gentle Clare!"
　　"Alas!" she said, "the while,
Oh, think of your immortal weal!
In vain for Constance is your zeal;
　　She—died at Holy Isle."
Lord Marmion started from the ground,
As light as if he felt no wound;
Though in the action burst the tide
In torrents, from his wounded side.

"Then it was truth," he said—"I knew
That the dark presage must be true.
I would the Fiend, to whom belongs
The vengeance due to all her wrongs
    Would spare me but a day!
For wasting fire, and dying groan,
And priests slain on the altar stone
    Might bribe him for delay.
It may not be!—this dizzy trance—
Curse on yon base marauder's lance,
And doubly cursed my failing brand!
A sinful heart makes feeble hand."
Then, fainting, down on earth he sunk
Supported by the trembling monk.

XXXII

With fruitless labour, Clara bound,
And strove to staunch the gushing wound:
The monk with unavailing cares,
Exhausted all the Church's prayers.
Ever, he said, that, close and near,
A lady's voice was in his ear,
And that the priest he could not hear;
    For that she ever sung,
"In the lost battle, borne down by the flying
Where mingles war's rattle with groans of the dying!"
    So the notes rung;—
"Avoid thee, Fiend!—with cruel hand,
Shake not the dying sinner's sand!
Oh, look, my son, upon yon sign
Of the Redeemer's grace divine!
    Oh, think on faith and bliss!
By many a death-bed I have been,
And many a sinner's parting seen,
    But never aught like this."
The war, that for a space did fail,
Now trebly thundering swelled the gale
    And—"Stanley!" was the cry;

A light on Marmion's visage spread,
    And fired his glazing eye:
With dying hand, above his head,
He shook the fragment of his blade,
    And shouted "Victory!
Charge, Chester, charge! On, Stanley, on!"
Were the last words of Marmion.

XXXIII

By this, though deep the evening fell,
Still rose the battle's deadly swell,
For still the Scots, around their king,
Unbroken, fought in desperate ring.
Where's now their victor vaward wing,
    Where Huntly, and where Home?
Oh, for a blast of that dread horn,
On Fontarabian echoes borne,
    That to King Charles did come,
When Rowland brave, and Olivier,
And every paladin and peer,
    On Roncesvalles died!
Such blast might warn them, not in vain,
To quit the plunder of the slain,
And turn the doubtful day again,
    While yet on Flodden side,
Afar, the royal standard flies,
And round it toils, and bleeds, and dies,
    Our Caledonian pride!
In vain the wish—for far away,
While spoil and havoc mark their way,
Near Sybil's Cross the plunderers stray.
"Oh, lady," cried the monk, "away!"
    And placed her on her steed,
And led her to the chapel fair,
    Of Tillmouth upon Tweed.
There all the night they spent in prayer,
And at the dawn of morning, there
She met her kinsman, Lord Fitz-Clare.

XXXIV

But as they left the dark'ning heath,
More desperate grew the strife of death.
The English shafts in volleys hailed,
In headlong charge their horse assailed;
Front, flank, and rear, the squadrons sweep
To break the Scottish circle deep,
  That fought around their king.
But yet, though thick the shafts as snow,
Though charging knights like whirlwinds go,
Though billmen ply the ghastly blow,
  Unbroken was the ring;
The stubborn spearmen still made good
Their dark impenetrable wood,
Each stepping where his comrade stood,
  The instant that he fell.
No thought was there of dastard flight;
Linked in the serried phalanx tight,
Groom fought like noble, squire like knight,
  As fearlessly and well;
Till utter darkness closed her wing
O'er their thin host and wounded king.
Then skilful Surrey's sage commands
Led back from strife his shattered bands;
  And from the charge they drew,
As mountain-waves, from wasted lands,
  Sweep back to ocean blue.
Then did their loss his foemen know;
Their king, their lords, their mightiest low,
They melted from the field as snow,
When streams are swoll'n and south winds blow,
  Dissolves in silent dew.
Tweed's echoes heard the ceaseless plash,
  While many a broken band,
Disordered, through her currents dash,
  To gain the Scottish land;
To town and tower, to down and dale,
To tell red Flodden's dismal tale,

And raise the universal wail.
Tradition, legend, tune, and song,
Shall many an age that wail prolong:
Still from the sire the son shall hear
Of the stern strife, and carnage drear,
    Of Flodden's fatal field,
Where shivered was fair Scotland's spear,
    And broken was her shield!

XXXV

Day dawns upon the mountain's side:—
There, Scotland! lay thy bravest pride,
Chiefs, knights, and nobles, many a one:
The sad survivors all are gone.
View not that corpse mistrustfully,
Defaced and mangled though it be;
Nor to yon Border castle high,
Look northward with upbraiding eye;
    Nor cherish hope in vain,
That, journeying far on foreign strand,
The royal pilgrim to his land
    May yet return again.
He saw the wreck his rashness wrought;
Reckless of life, he desperate fought,
    And fell on Flodden plain:
And well in death his trusty brand,
Firm clenched within his manly hand,
    Beseemed the monarch slain.
But, oh! how changed since yon blithe night!
Gladly I turn me from the sight,
    Unto my tale again.

XXXVI

Short is my tale:—Fitz-Eustace' care
A pierced and mangled body bare
To moated Lichfield's lofty pile;
And there, beneath the southern aisle,

A tomb, with Gothic sculpture fair,
Did long Lord Marmion's image bear,
(Now vainly for its site you look;
'Twas levelled, when fanatic Brook
The fair cathedral stormed and took;
But, thanks to Heaven, and good Saint Chad,
A guerdon meet the spoiler had!)
There erst was martial Marmion found,
His feet upon a couchant hound,
    His hands to heaven upraised;
And all around, on scutcheon rich,
And tablet carved, and fretted niche,
    His arms and feats were blazed.
And yet, though all was carved so fair,
And priest for Marmion breathed the prayer,
The last Lord Marmion lay not there.
From Ettrick woods, a peasant swain
Followed his lord to Flodden plain—
One of those flowers, whom plaintive lay
In Scotland mourns as "wede away;"
Sore wounded, Sybil's Cross he spied,
And dragged him to its foot, and died,
Close by the noble Marmion's side.
The spoilers stripped and gashed the slain,
And thus their corpses were mista'en;
And thus, in the proud baron's tomb,
The lowly woodsman took the room.

XXXVII

Less easy task it were, to show
Lord Marmion's nameless grave, and low.
    They dug his grave e'en where he lay,
        But every mark is gone:
    Time's wasting hand has done away
    The simple cross of Sybil Gray,
        And broke her font of stone;
But yet out from the little hill
Oozes the slender springlet still.

Oft halts the stranger there,
For thence may best his curious eye
The memorable field descry;
And shepherd boys repair
To seek the water-flag and rush,
And rest them by the hazel bush,
     And plait their garlands fair;
Nor dream they sit upon the grave
That holds the bones of Marmion brave.
When thou shalt find the little hill,
With thy heart commune, and be still.
If ever, in temptation strong,
Thou left'st the right path for the wrong;
If every devious step, thus trod,
Still led thee further from the road;
Dread thou to speak presumptuous doom
On noble Marmion's lowly tomb;
But say, "He died a gallant knight,
With sword in hand, for England's right."

XXXVIII

I do not rhyme to that dull elf,
Who cannot image to himself,
That, all through Flodden's dismal night,
Wilton was foremost in the fight;
That when brave Surrey's steed was slain,
'Twas Wilton mounted him again;
'Twas Wilton's brand that deepest hewed,
Amid the spearmen's stubborn wood:
Unnamed by Holinshed or Hall,
He was the living soul of all;
That, after fight, his faith made plain,
He won his rank and lands again;
And charged his old paternal shield
With bearings won on Flodden Field.
Nor sing I to that simple maid,
To whom it must in terms be said,
That king and kinsmen did agree,

To bless fair Clara's constancy;
Who cannot, unless I relate,
Paint to her mind the bridal's state;
That Wolsey's voice the blessing spoke,
More, Sands, and Denny, passed the joke:
That bluff King Hal the curtain drew,
And Katherine's hand the stocking threw;
And afterwards, for many a day,
That it was held enough to say,
In blessing to a wedded pair,
"Love they like Wilton and like Clare!"

L'envoy

To the Reader

Why then a final note prolong,
Or lengthen out a closing song,
Unless to bid the gentles speed,
Who long have listed to my rede?
To statesmen grave, if such may deign
To read the minstrel's idle strain,
Sound head, clean hand, and piercing wit,
And patriotic heart—as Pitt!
A garland for the hero's crest,
And twined by her he loves the best.
To every lovely lady bright,
What can I wish but faithful knight?
To every faithful lover too,
What can I wish but lady true?
And knowledge to the studious sage;—
And pillow to the head of age.
To thee, dear schoolboy, whom my lay
Has cheated of thy hour of play,
Light task, and merry holiday!
To all, to each, a fair good night,
And pleasing dreams, and slumbers light!

A Note About the Author

Sir Walter Scott (1771–1832) was a Scottish novelist, poet, playwright, and historian who also worked as a judge and legal administrator. Scott's extensive knowledge of history and his exemplary literary technique earned him a role as a prominent author of the romantic movement and innovator of the historical fiction genre. After rising to fame as a poet, Scott started to venture into prose fiction as well, which solidified his place as a popular and widely-read literary figure, especially in the 19th century. Scott left behind a legacy of innovation, and is praised for his contributions to Scottish culture.

A Note from the Publisher

Spanning many genres, from non-fiction essays to literature classics to children's books and lyric poetry, Mint Edition books showcase the master works of our time in a modern new package. The text is freshly typeset, is clean and easy to read, and features a new note about the author in each volume. Many books also include exclusive new introductory material. Every book boasts a striking new cover, which makes it as appropriate for collecting as it is for gift giving. Mint Edition books are only printed when a reader orders them, so natural resources are not wasted. We're proud that our books are never manufactured in excess and exist only in the exact quantity they need to be read and enjoyed.

bookfinity™

Discover more of your favorite classics with Bookfinity™.

- Track your reading with custom book lists.
- Get great book recommendations for your personalized Reader Type.
- Add reviews for your favorite books.
- AND MUCH MORE!

Visit **bookfinity.com** and take the fun Reader Type quiz to get started.

Enjoy our classic and modern companion pairings!

Printed in the USA
CPSIA information can be obtained
at www.ICGtesting.com
JSHW022340140824
68134JS00019B/1602

9 781513 280332